Jim is one of America's most sought after presenters in the area of parenting and school discipline. His practical techniques are revolutionizing the way parents and professionals are looking at how we deal with children, how we help them become responsible, thinking people, and how we help them enhance their own self-concept.

FOSTER W. CLINE, M.D. is an internationally-renowned child and adult psychiatrist, lecturer and consultant, and father of three birth children, one adopted child and several foster children. He is also a grandparent.

Dr. Cline is the founder of Evergreen Consultants in Human Behavior, a multidisciplinary group of professionals visited by people from all over the world, for treatment of individual and family problems. The group specializes in treatment of severely disturbed children and adolescents.

Dr. Cline lectures extensively and is also very popular as a psychiatric consultant to school systems, pupil personnel teams and hospitals throughout the world.

Dr. Cline is a prolific author. He has written several books, including *Parenting With Love and Logic, Parenting Teens With Love and Logic, Grandparenting with Love and Logic* (co-authored with Jim Fay) and *Conscienceless Acts, Societal Mayhem,* some twenty professional papers, numerous articles as well as audio and video tapes. Foster has an uncanny ability to share his ideas and expertise in such a way that readers and audiences immediately envision themselves being more successful with young people. This practical and immediate help, coupled with his dynamic presentation style, has placed him in high demand as a speaker.

Foster has received many honors, including the Special Award for Outstanding Contributions to Children by the National Conference of the North American Council of Adoptive Children.

The Pearls of Love and Logic for Parents and Teachers

*I'm starting to use Love and Logic pearls on my family.
The principles are common sense and easy to use tools to teach children
that they are loveable, capable and responsible.*

LESLYE ERZBERGER
Parent
Lino Lakes, Minnesota

*I feel fortunate to have discovered the practical, uncomplicated advice found
in Love and Logic so early in my teaching career. I use the strategies daily
and am often stunned by the positive results.*

AMITY DUETTRA
Olalla Elementary School
Olalla, Washington

*Being an elementary school principal is finally fun. By employing the philosophies
of Love and Logic, the kids do all the work and I get to enjoy their thinking process.
Watching them grow to be responsible students is very exciting.*

JUDY L. SPARKMAN
Principal, Town Center Elementary School
Coppell, Texas

*The discipline strategies and "can do" attitudes learned from Love and Logic
have helped students to be actively engaged in learning and problem solving.
I'm excited to think that* Pearls of Love and Logic for Parents and Teachers *can be
the bridge to helping parents reinforce the skills their children practice at school.*

JUDITH A. GRISWOLD, PH.D.
Principal, Park Lane Elementary School
Aurora, Colorado

*Do you want kids to be successful and responsible? Do you want to feel more successful
as a parent or teacher? If you answered "Yes" to either question, then you must read*
Pearls of Love and Logic for Parents and Teachers.

CORWIN KRONENBERGER
Consultant, Educator, Presenter
Bloomington, Minnesota

*Great idea! The "Pearls" give practical advice that is easily read.
Parents and/or teachers can pick up this book and read one "pearl" at a time
and receive great information without a huge time commitment.*

JEANNETTE FRENCH
Certified Becoming a Love and Logic Parent Facilitator
Columbia, Missouri

*Love and Logic Pearls provides clear, concise, easy to apply techniques
that make for more peaceful classrooms and lower volume levels at home.
I have witnessed Love and Logic principles transform the lives of parents,
teachers, administrators, and most importantly, the children they influence.*

LARRY ANDERSON
Parent and Principal
Sioux Falls, South Dakota

*A perfect book for parents and teachers who wonder"Now that I've got them,
what do I do with them?"* Pearls of Love and Logic for Parents and Teachers
*has wonderful "at your fingertip" advice for parents and teachers who,
after one year or eighteen years, want to say, "I did a good job!"*

SHAUNA AGNEW
Certified Becoming a Love and Logic Parent Facilitator, Parent, Grandparent
Las Vegas, Nevada

Introduction

"HEY, JIM, OL' BUDDY. How about writing some of those articles for us? We could copy them into our newsletters. Save us a lot of time. Make us look good to the parents. How about it?"

These were some of my school principal friends trying to get me to do their work for them. They were referring to the monthly articles I wrote for our school newsletter. I'm not sure they realized that one of my most enjoyable tasks as a school principal was to write the monthly newsletter. The part I enjoyed best was writing my articles about raising responsible children, titled *Principally Speaking*.

When I found out that my principal friends were serious, I started sharing these articles. This became possible through the advent of desktop publishing. Parents seemed so appreciative that I decided that when I left the schools and had some time, I would provide these articles in a form that could be used by school principals nationwide.

It was not long before The Cline/Fay Love and Logic Institute was making available more than 100 different articles. My partner, Foster W. Cline, M.D., was now contributing his writings. The program for distributing these soon became known as *Special Thoughts on Raising Kids*. Our best calculations indicate that over half a million people were introduced to Love and Logic® through these articles as they appeared in school newsletters.

As our Love and Logic Institute grew, followers of Love and Logic continually asked for reprints of these articles. Phone requests such as, "We need more of these short, to the point, practical articles," were taken each day. Customer service staff members found themselves constantly

running to the filing cabinets looking for specific articles and trying to satisfy the growing number of requests.

During a recent conference, one of the Love and Logic Parent Trainers came to me with an idea. "Jim, tell you what you need to do. You need to take a whole stack of those articles and print them into one book so people can have them all."

My first thought was, "Oh, wow! Why didn't I ever think of that? We can do it." That very week plans were laid for the creation of this book. Thanks to Carol Thomas, our coordinator of product development, and her staff, The Love and Logic Pearls of Jim Fay and Foster W. Cline, M.D. is a reality. If you enjoy reading them as much as we enjoyed writing them, we are all winners.

Enjoy,

Jim Fay

JIM FAY. *President*
Cline/Fay Love and Logic Institute, Inc.

Contents

Chapter
One

1

My Child, the Winner

THE GREATEST GIFT WE CAN GIVE children is the knowledge that they can first rely on themselves for the answers to their problems. A child who develops an attitude that says, "I can probably find my own solutions, and if not, adults will be willing to give me some advice," becomes a survivor. This child usually has the edge in learning, relating to others, and making his or her way in the world.

People often ask how they can support their children to ensure they excel. This often means, "What can I do to make sure my child gets ahead or is a winner?" Sometimes it means, "What can I do to help my child be successful, feel secure, and lead a happy life?" It doesn't matter which question is asked. The answer is the same.

The foundation for success lies in the belief that the best solution to any problem comes from within. Then if you don't find the answers, ask for advice from others.

Parents and teachers can help children develop this attitude by being understanding and sympathetic each time a child has a problem. This can be expressed in a variety of ways such as, "I bet that really bothers you," or "Wow! I bet that makes you feel mad," or "If that happened to me, I would really feel . . ."

These types of statements usually bring about some kind of response that conveys that the child is relieved that we understand. As soon as we see that response, it is time to ask one of the most important questions children ever hear, "What do you think you are going to do about it?" This is a powerful statement because it implies that we know the child is capable of doing his or her own thinking.

This question is often answered by, "I don't know." This is a good time to offer some different kinds of solutions. We discuss the possible consequences with the youngster and then allow the child to choose the solution he/she likes best, even if it means that the child decides not to solve his/her problem.

Children have too few opportunities to learn about and practice for the real world. These opportunities present themselves most often as problems to solve or decisions to make. Each time I move into the situation, solve the problem, or rescue the child, *I have stolen one of the child's growth experiences.* He or she is now less prepared to face the real world than if I had been there with understanding and the question, "What are you going to do about it?"

❤

STEPS
1. Show understanding.
2. Ask, "How are you going to solve the problem?"
3. Share some choices.
4. Help him/her look at the consequences.
5. Give the child permission to solve it or not solve it.

2

A Computer with a Lifetime Guarantee

BARRY NEIL KAUFFMAN, one of our leading psychologists, says, "The way to change a person's behavior is to first change the way he sees the world." He tells us that people do the very best they can considering the way they see themselves and the way they see the world.

Other leading psychologists tell us the same thing in another way. They say our behavior is controlled by our self-concept. They say to change our behavior, we must first change our self-concept. Self-concept is a very important part of our lives. Its discovery is one of the great breakthroughs in psychology. Dennis Waitley describes the importance of self-concept when he discusses two levels of the mind, the conscious and the subconscious. The conscious level works much like a judge, collecting and evaluating information.

The subconscious level functions much like a computer. It stores information and makes it available at a later date. The subconscious never attempts to sort out fact from fiction or truth from misperception. When information flows from the subconscious, it comes forth as fact. Therefore, all our misperceptions, eventually become truth and are treated as fact by the conscious level of the mind.

Children work very hard at trying to understand their parents as well as their environment. They are great observers, but horrible interpreters. This is understandable considering their immature brains and limited experience. The sad part is when we become adults and look back, all of our perceptions, both accurate and inaccurate, become our reality.

A child who has a misperception that his parents prefer his brother does not grow up to say to his parents, "When I was young I thought you loved my brother more than you loved me." He grows up to say, "You always liked my brother more than you liked me!" What was once his mistaken idea has now become his truth.

A child is constantly observing, interpreting, and storing information in the subconscious. These billions of thoughts and experiences later become the truth that runs and directs his or her life. The challenge is to help a child interpret what he or she sees and hears in ways that can be used later as proof that he or she is capable, lovable, and responsible.

I often wonder what mistaken beliefs and interpretations have been stored in the subconscious minds of youngsters who constantly make poor decisions, involve themselves in self-destructive behaviors, or turn off learning. It makes me wonder how many of these people have misinterpreted their parents' love in the following ways:

1. Some parents show love by hovering over and rescuing their child from the harsh world. This is often interpreted by the child as, "My parents know that I could never handle this world without help." I am not capable.

2. Some parents show love through control. These parents constantly tell children how to lead their lives. This is often interpreted as, "My parents know that I am not capable of thinking for myself or being responsible." I am not capable.

3. Some parents show love by always being available with advice. They allow their children to make many of their own decisions. This is often interpreted as, "My parents know that I can think for myself!" These children grow up to believe that somewhere within themselves is a computer with a lifetime guarantee.

❤

MY GIFT TO YOU:
You are lovable, capable, responsible

3

Anger vs. Empathy

I FEEL SAD FOR CHILDREN who are so controlled that they seldom make mistakes. They are the disadvantaged ones. The children who make poor choices from time to time are the ones who get to learn more about the real world and how it works.

Most of us can look back and see that many of the important lessons we learned were a result of the mistakes we made. The lessons learned best were those in which our parents allowed us to suffer the consequences of our mistakes. These were the times when our parents used more actions than words.

Example: Jennifer often forgets to take her homework to school. She calls home to ask her mother to bring the assignments to school, saying, "Gee, Mom, you don't want me to get a bad grade do you?"

Jennifer's loving mother takes the homework to school, usually with a reprimand: "How many times have I told you that I'm not going to bring this to you anymore?" This mother is giving Jennifer *"forgetting lessons"* by rescuing her. She is using meaningless words and not actions. Her anger is teaching Jennifer that Mom will get angry, but it is not teaching Jennifer to remember her homework.

Let's suppose that Mom changes her approach to this problem and allows the natural consequences to fall. She will be understanding when Jennifer calls and asks her to bring her homework to school. Her answer will be, "I'm sorry, Jennifer, but I'm not available to do that for you." She will use as few words as possible because she knows that children often use our words against us. Jennifer will probably try arguing, "Now I'm going to get a bad grade and it's all your fault!"

Mom knows that the best way to argue with a child is not to argue. "That may be true. I'm sorry you forgot your homework. I'll see you when you get home. Have the best day possible under the circumstances."

Mom's action in this case will provide *"remembering lessons."* The words she used tell what she will do and how sorry she feels for Jennifer. This mother is using empathy and understanding instead of anger and lectures.

Mistakes or Opportunities?

Our children frequently make mistakes that hurt them. As parents, we have two possible ways of reacting when this happens. One is to use anger and lectures. The other is to use understanding or empathy. Each of these reactions does its own special job of teaching.

It is easy for us to see which is the best. However, it is important to remember that sometimes our grandparents, parents, or teachers taught us through their actions to use anger.

If we saw and heard anger as a child, our hardest job in parenting is overcoming this influence.

Those who are best at this plan ahead. They know that it is difficult to change in the "heat of battle" or when feelings are at a high pitch. Practice and rehearse new actions during quiet times so you can come across in new and surprising ways to your youngster. It's fun to be the one who is in control.

❤

ANGER teaches children to look at the adult's anger
EMPATHY teaches children to look at their lives and decisions

4

Inflation

KIDS SUFFER FROM INFLATION. The cost of learning how to live in our world goes up daily. The price a child pays today to learn about friendships, school, learning, decision making, and responsibility is the cheapest it will ever be. Learning an important lesson today may be a bargain.

The older a child gets, the bigger the decisions become. Elementary school children make many decisions with affordable price tags. This means they can pick themselves up and try again if things don't work out. High school students are making life-and-death decisions—about fast cars, riding in the back of pickup trucks, drugs, alcohol, and other issues—on a daily basis.

Some children are allowed to learn at an early age not to antagonize bigger children. The cost of this knowledge is a few minor bumps and bruises. Others, protected from this experience, have to learn the same lesson during their teenage years at the cost of serious physical injury, usually at the hands of a much stronger person. I'd rather my child learn at an early age when the price is much more affordable.

I met a parent who likes to loan money to her young children. She believes this is a great opportunity for them to learn about responsibility and the way our banking system works.

She expects the child to sign a promissory note, provide collateral just as an adult would do at the bank, and pay off the loan by a certain date. She is actually training and preparing her children for the real world. Recently she repossessed a tape recorder when her son did not pay off his loan on time. She said that it really hurt her to have to take the tape recorder.

However, her most convincing statement was, "My son is really lucky. Here he is, only 10 years old, and he knows so much about the responsibility of paying back loans, collateral, and even repossessions. All it cost him was a $29 tape recorder. It was a bargain."

She added, "My neighbor's boy learned the same lesson at the age of 26 when the bank repossessed his $2,900 car. My son had a 16-year head start on the neighbor boy. Now he has an additional piece of wisdom to carry him through life." His life will be better in the long run as a result of this lesson.

It's painful to watch our children learn through natural consequences. But that pain is the price we pay to teach our children.

We either hurt as we watch our children learn through life's natural consequences, or we hurt as we watch them grow up unable to take good care of themselves.

❤

Allow Kids to Learn When the Price Is Affordable
I guess no one said it was going to be easy

5

Self-Concept

I'M NOT HELD BACK because of what I can't do. I'm held back because of what I'm afraid I can't do. More often, I am held back because of my fear that I might fail, and as a result, I might not like myself. That's called lack of self-esteem.

Our self-concept rules our lives. It sometimes works as a wonderful encourager and sometimes as a tyrannical dictator, controlling almost every move we make, it talks to us constantly, "You can do it. Go for it!" or, "Not me. I could never do that."

Our self-concept lives at the subconscious level of thinking, over which we have little control. It grew there when we were little children and continues to grow and change with every new experience. The subconscious mind stores every experience just like a computer.

However, computers have no ability to decide right from wrong, fact from fiction. Everything stored in the computer later comes out as fact. In computerland this is known as "garbage in, garbage out."

Our subconscious mind does the same thing. It cannot tell the difference between things we vividly imagine and things that really happen. As a result, everything that is stored comes out as fact, even when the original source is imagination or misunderstanding.

A youngster's mind is especially receptive to what is going on in his or her world. The self-concept computer is not firmly set. Therefore, children are easily influenced by the messages they think they hear from their parents and teachers. We can help children store positive or negative messages. We do the best job of this, not through our words, but through our actions.

Parents and teachers who constantly encourage children to decide between two alternatives teach children to think for themselves. They send powerful messages that imply, "You are so smart that I can allow you to think for yourself." This action also implies, "I can trust you to know what is good for you."

Wise parents usually suggest two choices in a manner that allow them to be happy with either choice. An example of this is: "Our car will be leaving for town in 20 minutes. Are you going to wear your coat or carry it? It's your choice."

Some parents give orders, such as "You wear your coat or else!" This sends a *"you're dumb"* message. After a period of time these parents discover using too many orders has caused their child's low self-concept.

A child's self-concept is the sum total of all the *"you're smart"* messages he or she hears minus all the *"you're dumb"* messages. Hopefully, our actions send more positive messages than negative ones.

❤

Kids Look at Our Actions to Learn Who They Are

6

Love Is First

JIM FAY, PRESIDENT OF CLINE/FAY INSTITUTE, INC., shares a sad but important story about his life.

He wasn't much of a student when he was growing up. This was a great concern to his mother. Being a loving mother, she became very involved in helping him improve. This meant spending a lot of time with him after school drilling him on his reading and math.

His dad got into the act by making sure that he read every night and that he was never caught reading comic books. Dad said comic books made children like him lazy and silly instead of serious and studious.

As he looks back on it, he understands the things his parents did were right for their times. They were done out of their love for him. His mother and father made many sacrifices, especially with their time.

Unfortunately, he read much of what they did in the wrong way. Like most kids, he was insecure and was always looking for proof that his parents loved and accepted him.

He especially looked for things like smiles, eye contact, and touching. Unfortunately, these things had to wait because his parents were so determined to help him succeed.

As a result, he developed the view that people are loved only when they do a good job. He has experienced many unhappy times as a result of this irrational belief.

Insights for Jim

Recently Jim was involved in an interview with some high school students who had been working their way out of drug problems. One

of the questions to these youngsters was, "Is there anything the adults in your life could have done to help you avoid this problem?"

The answer hit home for him. All the students said that youngsters are recognized and made to feel loved when they are straight "A" students, but they did not feel that the adults recognized and loved them for who they were.

They all said that as a result of their not being top students, they began to feel left out. They felt it would have been easier for them if there had been at least one person who showed love and acceptance regardless of their abilities and achievements.

Solutions

Jim thinks that his parents could have made their love clearer to him while helping him improve his schoolwork.

It might have been better if they had told Jim they were helping so they could feel good about their own responsibilities and so he would feel good about himself.

He could have heard a strong message about their love if they had told him it would still be there even when he was having trouble in school. Additional help might have resulted if they had relaxed more about his schoolwork and made more time for some smiles and hugs.

Jim now knows that the children who have the most difficulty in school are the ones who most need parents who say, "Let's forget about school now that you are home. We can love and enjoy you regardless of your school problems." This helps children "recharge" their batteries so they can feel stronger and more willing to go back and try it again.

❤

You Are Loved Not for What You Do But for Who You Are

7

The Science of Control

MANY PARENTS SPEND A LOT OF TIME trying to take control of their children's actions. This is natural. It is easy to feel like bad parents when we see our children out of control.

There is nothing more pathetic to see than a child out of control. This scares parents and children alike. A child who knows that he is out of control feels insecure. He puts on a tough exterior. His actions are easy to misread because they appear as attempts to show that he cannot, and will not, be controlled. He needs limits but often fights having them.

Parents can set limits in these situations by giving away some of their control. At the same time they will be gaining more control. This small miracle comes about when children are given choices rather than orders.

It is also refreshing to know that the same technique reduces stress in families while preparing children to make decisions that affect them as they go through their lives. It provides wonderful preparation for the real world in which they will have to live.

Consider this situation in which a parent gives some control to the child while gaining more for himself. A youngster is making too much noise in the family room. A typical parental response might be, "Quit making so much noise. You're making me mad!"

This usually does not work since it gives the child the wrong kind of control. He now feels he has the power to make his parent mad.

This parent gives the child some positive control over his own life by offering choices: "You can either stay here with us being quiet, or go somewhere else to make your noise."

A determined youngster might fight this by saying, "I'm staying here! I have just as many rights as you do!" The parent's calm reply is simply, "That's not one of the choices, but feel welcome to come back with us when the noises are finished."

Providing choices is based upon the fact that most people cannot make decisions about themselves and fight with others at the same time. Parents can easily set the limits children need by taking good care of themselves at the same time they offer the choices. The parent in this last example sets limits regarding the child's behavior around others without putting the child down.

The youngster's dignity was maintained as he was left with a decision regarding his behavior. The parent's dignity was maintained as he handled the situation in a calm, controlled manner.

Effective parents offer choices only when they are willing to ensure that their children will live with the consequences of their choices. These parents know that children need to learn from their mistakes. Mistakes are often better teachers than parents who lecture.

❤

Allow Me to Learn from My Mistakes

8

Room to Grow

ONE OF THE MORE GLARING PROBLEMS faced by teenagers in today's world occurs when their parents become determined to control every aspect of their lives.

This control can be seen as a symptom of a larger problem that actually belongs to the parent. It is a problem that many of us face. We feel insecure when we have little control over others, especially our children.

Since we never like to admit to ourselves that we are insecure, we build a case for being concerned about the youngster's well-being at an unconscious level. This is a very natural thing to do.

As we state our case, it comes out as, "I need to control my youngster's actions, or he will do something that will be bad for him, and my love for him just won't allow me to do otherwise."

The way we identify insecurity is by watching the amount of control a person needs to have over others. This is seen daily as parents attempt to control sleeping and eating habits, the amount of learning that takes place, the language used by the child, how he or she is treated by others, the kind of clothes he or she wears, and who his or her friends are.

We don't hear a person say, "Well, actually, I'm a very controlling person because I feel like an inadequate parent when my child makes decisions for himself and chooses to be something different than what I have designed for him." Our minds work for us as a protection from these kinds of thoughts.

Instead we hear, "I care about my children. I can't let them hurt themselves by making bad choices" or, "I just don't want my chil-

dren to close any doors for themselves that will limit their opportunities later in life."

In other words, controlling people unconsciously disguise their attempts to feel more adequate by saying that they are caring, concerned, involved, and so on.

The question is, "Do I feel secure enough to allow my child to become what he or she wants to be?"

❤

*CONTROL helps parents satisfy unconscious needs
to feel more adequate as adults.*

*DEMANDS TO GET YOUR WAY help youngsters learn
to be stubborn and demand to get their way.*

*CHOICES help children learn to become decision makers
and learn to become adults in the real world.*

9

Schoolwork

YOU'RE ON YOUR WAY HOME FROM WORK. You're anxious for some encouraging talk and a little relaxation after a hard day. You need all the support you can get to recharge your batteries and feel strong enough to go back tomorrow and face another working day.

You are greeted with, "Hi, Honey. How was it today? Where are your papers? I want to see how you did today."

"It was OK," you reply. "I really don't want to talk about it; I'm really beat."

"Well, no wonder you don't want to talk about it. Look at these papers. You can do a lot better than this. Where was your mind today? You sit down right now and we'll go over these proposals you wrote and get the spelling straightened out. And look at these paragraphs. You'll never get promoted at this rate. I don't understand this. You have so much more potential than this."

How long would it be before you find a more comfortable place to go after work? "Who needs this?" you'll say. "I can find someone who can show me a little more appreciation for my hard work!"

Many school-age children face this same situation daily. They are greeted after school with, "What did you learn today?" and "Where is your homework? You get on it right now!"

Children are also requested to bring home their papers so that the mistakes can be corrected. Even though this is done with love and caring, it trains them to focus on their weaknesses.

The problem faced by students is that they can't choose to go somewhere else after school. They can't avoid facing a replay of their daily failures. They must return home and listen to whatever their parents have to say. It is very difficult for a child to say, "Mother! Do you realize you

are training me to keep my school progress a secret from you?" Soon they quit bringing home papers. They make excuses and blame it on their teachers. "She never gives me my papers to bring home."

The next step is for the parent to go to school demanding that the teacher develop some sort of foolproof reporting method. Teachers are actually faced with writing daily and weekly reports for parents. This never provides a long-term solution because it addresses the wrong problem. It also robs teachers of valuable teaching and preparation time.

The real problem is that the child has learned that it is unsafe to discuss school with his or her parents. Rather than developing a reporting plan, it is much wiser to work on the real problem—helping children and parents learn to talk to each other in safe and supportive ways. This solution works, and it lasts a lifetime.

You can teach your child to discuss school with you. While you are doing this, you can also lay the foundation blocks that will build a true winner out of your youngster.

Winners always think about how they are going to succeed. Losers always think about their possible failures.

STEP ONE: Sit down with your children two to three times per week. Have them point out the best things they did on their papers.

STEP TWO: Make sure your child describes to you the reasons for his or her success. As they put these into words, the reasons for the success will be imprinted on their brain, never to be erased. They will start to believe they are in control of their success.

STEP THREE: Work with your children on their mistakes only when they ask for your help. Let the school work on deficiencies. Teachers have training to help with the deficiencies in effective ways.

STEP FOUR: Be patient. This is a real change in operation. It will take the child a period of time to believe that this is not just a new phase his parents are going through. Look for the real benefits to show up in several months or maybe during the next few years, depending upon the child's past history.

WINNERS focus on their strengths
LOSERS focus on their weaknesses

10

Grades

OUR KIDS ARE STARTING SCHOOL. It won't be long until we get their report cards, right? Wrong! *We* don't get the report cards—*they* do! That's the point. In fact, it brings us to the first rule about handling report cards:

Keep the monkey on your child's back

It's important that students know report cards are their business. As parents, we care. Our caring might even border on concern. But worrying? That's your child's business.

Foster W. Cline, M.D. often talks about how his wise old dad always kept the report card problem on his back. As a young child, Foster had a severe learning disorder, usually bringing home straight D's on his report card. Looking over the report card, his father would always poise his fat black fountain pen, and inevitably ask, "Son, are you proud of this?" Foster would then reply, "No, Sir." And then Dad would say, "That's good, Son," and sign the report card. Heaven help Foster if he ever said he was proud of the report card.

Wise Mr. Cline knew that when a child performs like a "turkey," he often wishes to become an "eagle." But when a child performs like a "turkey" and feels like an "eagle," he won't fly very far!

Show more excitement about high grades than low grades— Children want pizzazz. They crave parental emotion. On an unconscious level, surprisingly, it doesn't matter whether the parental emotion surrounds great things or poor things. Children always shoot for emotion.

A parent handling the situation might say, "Hey! A big 'A' in art! Wow, a 'B' in gym. Well, of course, you always did run like the wind. Hey, a big 'B' in typing. You'll probably be able to turn out papers quickly. That's important. Humm, a 'D' in math. Well, I suppose that could be better. Wow, a big 'B' in social studies. It's important to know history!" Then nonemotionally ask, "How are you going to handle the math?"

Poor grades are not the problem—The reason for the poor grades is the problem— Students receive poor grades because of poor self-images, rebelliousness against parental value systems, anxiety, depression, learning problems, and a host of other reasons.

Sometimes the reason is an attitude problem, and sometimes we need to accept that. One evening, for example, Foster's daughter had an attitude problem. She said, "I hate algebra. I'm not going to look at the problems. I'm not going to even do my homework!" Such a poor attitude, out of character for Robin, surprised him. In his parental wisdom, he replied, "Well, Robin, your attitude surprises me. Would you like some help on your algebra tonight?" She brightened right up, answering, "Oh sure, Dad. Thanks!"

Foster tried an algebra problem, and finally worked out an answer. He was pretty proud of himself until Robin checked his answer with the one in the back of the book. He had forgotten that some of these books actually provide the answers to the problems. His answer was *dead wrong!*

He worked the problem again. The answer was wrong again. A half an hour later he said, "I hate algebra! I never liked it! I've always had problems with it. Shut the darn book! Ask your teacher how to do it tomorrow! At that point he realized how difficult it can be to maintain a positive attitude when taking on a tough assignment.

❤

We Don't Get Report Cards, Kids Do

Chapter Two

11

Teen Underachievement

MOST PARENTS WANT THEIR TEENS to make it to the head of the class. Unfortunately, some teens lack the motivation to achieve good grades or even stay in school.

The reasons for underachievement can include low self-esteem, boredom, family issues, rebellion, and drug abuse. And, it is a rare teen who does not tire of the intense competition of high school at some point before graduation.

Self-Image—The Best Guarantee

A healthy self-image is by far the best guarantee for graduation. Our goal should be to help our children feel good about themselves, not force them to complete high school. Trying to motivate an underachieving teen through pressure doesn't work. Even if we were successful in keeping our teens in school, many would most likely fail their first semester of college or at their job.

We can help build self-esteem by keeping communication open, showing concern in place of anger and being available without rescuing.

Place Responsibility with Your Teen

When you try to force your teen to stay in school, the result is like forcing a child to eat chocolate, the child rebels in spite of himself!

It is essential that teens view their success or failure in school as their own responsibility. The parent in the following discussion sends this message:

DAD: "Larry, there are two ways we live our lives. One is preparing for life and the other is being in life. As long as you are preparing for life, I'm happy to pay room and board and tuition."

LARRY: "So?"

DAD: "So, your grades seem to indicate that you've quit preparing for life. Maybe it's time for you to pay your own way."

LARRY: "No, way! I'm going to graduate."

DAD: "If your grades are at least average next grading period, I'll know you are still preparing. If not, I'll know that you're in life and ready to pay your own way. I'll be interested to see what happens."

The responsibility for academic performance is now where it belongs—with Larry.

The Wrong Crowd

When teens run with a crowd that doesn't care about school, their grades often suffer. But forbidding teens from seeing their friends rarely works! It's better to maintain a good relationship with your teen, show concern without anger, and allow consequences to fall naturally.

What's Wrong with Being Average

Some parents are concerned when their teens bring home C's. No one likes to admit their children are average! But, in reality, many of us get C's in some areas of our lives. A little understanding goes a long way toward building self-esteem—the real issue behind underachievement.

❤

Low Self-Esteem and Low Self-Achievement Go Hand in Hand

12

Responsibility

I WATCHED A MAN AND HIS CHILDREN in the drug store the other day. One of his girls had a sad face while he yelled, "What's wrong with you? How many times have I told you to be responsible?"

Have you ever noticed that the parents who yell the loudest about responsibility seem to have the most irresponsible children? It is also true that many very responsible parents raise children who are not at all responsible.

The most responsible children usually come from families in which the word "responsibility" is rarely used. The mystery behind this has a lot to do with a concept in psychology that education consultant Jim Fay calls, the "No Sense in Both of Us Worrying about It" syndrome. He reminds us that most of us worry very little about something if someone else will do the worrying for us.

Jim writes that at one time he never worried about how money was spent because his wife, Shirley, was very responsible about saving. He used to say, "There's no sense in both of us worrying about that. Shirley has that well in hand." However, one day Shirley discovered that she enjoyed buying things. And wouldn't you guess, Jim started saying to himself, "Oh, oh! If she's not going to worry about that, somebody better!" He became a lot more concerned about money when she stopped being careful. Shirley trained him to be more concerned simply by being a lot less concerned.

So, there you have it. Parents who raise responsible kids do it through their actions, not their words. These parents go through life being responsible about their own jobs, demonstrating how it is done. At the same time, they spend very little time and energy worrying

about their children's responsibilities. They worry more about how to allow their children to experience the consequences of irresponsibility.

No Reminders— These parents are involved with their children, but do not spend their time reminding them or worrying for them. It is almost as if their attitudes are saying, "I'm sure you'll remember on your own, but if you don't, you'll surely learn something from the experience."

Reminders tell children we are afraid that they are not capable. Sad, but true, these implied messages have a lasting effect since children believe them without even realizing it.

Have you ever noticed that young people often live out their parents' deepest fears? Parents who constantly say, "Don't forget," raise children who forget. Those who say, "You show some respect," raise disrespectful children. Those who demand responsibility, raise kids who are irresponsible.

Consequences with Empathy— Responsible children are usually raised by parents who allow them to experience the consequences of irresponsible acts. These parents also help their children understand who owns the problem by being very sympathetic. "I'm sorry that worked out the way it did, I'm sure it's no fun having to do the job over again."

Most parents are pleasantly surprised to learn how effectively "consequences with understanding" develop responsibility.

❤

Replace Words with Meaningful Actions

13

Handling a Crisis

EVERY CRISIS IS DIFFERENT AND INDIVIDUAL, whether it's drug use, a runaway child, pregnancy, or a death in the family. Think of the Chinese character denoting crisis: it combines the symbols for danger and opportunity. It is important to see the opportunity in a crisis as well as the danger.

The most common mistake made during a crisis is to assume that something must be done right now! This is seldom the case. Here are four common elements that help us deal with a crisis:

1. Crises are often temporary— Remembering that this is a temporary problem helps us from becoming so anxious we become paralyzed or overinvolved. Many times a crisis is simply a long-term problem we haven't known about until now. If we suddenly discover we have cancer or our daughter is sexually involved with someone or our child has been taking drugs, *it's a big happening!* It certainly may be far from a *good* happening, but it's not necessarily a crisis.

2. Few crises need an immediate answer— Usually, there's time to seek advice from someone we respect, someone who has had similar experiences or who is a competent professional. It's also helpful to write down all of our options, including what would happen if we did nothing at all. This may not be the best solution, but at least it should be considered among all of our choices.

3. It's important to ask ourselves what would be the worst possible outcome— Once we can *state* the worst possible outcome, we also realize we can actually cope with it. It helps to ask, "Will we live through this?"

4. Always try to keep the monkey on the back of the person(s) responsible for the problem— If it's your teenager who has run away from home and is telephoning you for money, he or she may need to know they're welcome to return home. However, it's their responsibility to come up with the means of getting home, just as they figured out the means of running away. Parents may *loan* the teen money, backed up with collateral, in order to return home.

Remember, take a moment, breathe deeply, and relax. Write down all the possible choices, talk them over with a person you respect, and think about your ability to cope with the worst possible outcome.

❤

Ask Yourself: What Is the Worst Outcome?

14

Time for Bed

Sometimes bedtime can be a hassle. We say "Time for bed, Sweetie." And then what? Our children often have an exciting array of excuses to put us off: "I don't wanna," or "Can I have some ice cream first?" or "Read me a story."

This issue offers two guidelines for handling bedtime with children.

Don't "oversleep" your children— A friend remembers an early childhood filled with unnecessary naps. He and his brother would rub their eyes until they were red before stumbling out of their bedrooms in the afternoon. They would grope their way into their mom's room and say, "We just woke up. Can we get up now?" If they had wanted to get up because they weren't sleepy, it would not have been allowed.

Recent research indicates that bright children, particularly gifted children may not need as much sleep as others. Too bad. They are bright enough to be more of a problem when they are awake.

Some parents put their youngsters to bed simply to gain some time away from them. That's sad, because ideally children should be able to be up *and* unobtrusive at the same time! On the other hand, if adults need privacy in the evening, sending children to their *rooms* is more reasonable than sending them to *bed* early.

Understanding the child's reason for not wanting to go to bed— Sometimes younger children are afraid. Night is associated with scary noises and other strange things. Monsters are lords of the darkness. Every child knows that a night creature is not your basic

friendly puppy. Children have fairly active imaginations. One little eight-year-old girl, after recently being adopted, imagined that her parents only looked like humans. But at night, their skin would peel off and they were really lizards underneath. This sounds like a horror movie, but after all, horror stories touch something present within us all—things more readily accessible to children through their imaginations.

Explore your child's reasons for not wanting to go to sleep. For youngsters, going to bed is no fun if they know their parents fight as soon as they are out of sight. Fear of the dark, fear of loss, fear of the unknown, and fear of death may all play a role in a child's bedtime problems.

You can use simple, calm reassurance with the expectation that your child will be able to handle his or her own problems. Unfortunately, instead of providing simple reassurance, an overexploring or overly involved parent may sometimes elevate the ridiculous to the sublime. For example, pleading, "Ricky, you'll be all right, honey," makes things worse. And it definitely does not improve the situation when parents look under the bed to prove there are no monsters. Children are likely to be more afraid, thinking, "Wow! Maybe there are monsters or they would never be looking under the bed like that!"

If parents are relaxed and do not make a big issue out of bedtime, most youngsters will naturally go to bed when they get sleepy.

♥

Explore your child's reasons for not wanting to go to sleep

15

Adolescent Back Talk

AN ENLIGHTENED FATHER RECENTLY NOTED, "The more responsibility I give my son—without being overly protective—the nicer he is."

This parent has discovered that back talk ceases when we allow our teens enough opportunity to suffer and learn from their own mistakes. Generally, adolescents who talk back have parents who get angry and rescue them from the consequences of their actions.

There is hope for teens who display obnoxious, rebellious, and difficult behavior. The following explores ways to handle the three main reasons for back talk.

1. Teens talk back when we threaten their autonomy and independence— If your child was basically loving through the fifth or sixth grade, back talk usually clears up when you listen to your son or daughter's ideas and when you present your thoughts without trying to make your teen adopt your position. This approach provides your teen with love combined with the right to fail.

Teens may test us to see if we will rescue them. But most back talk ends after they find out we will only continue to lovingly provide our point of view in a non-angry way and allow them to suffer the consequences of their behavior.

A conversation that lets teens know they are responsible for their actions might go something like this:

MOM: "Robert, sometimes you and I have a difficult time together. How do you feel about this?"

ROBERT: "You're always on my case—you tell me what to do all the time. It makes me mad!"

MOM: "I know it does. I realize that I'm always trying to make sure you do the right thing and not get into trouble—but I'm not giving you the right to 'blow it' for yourself. I just wanted to apologize. Everyone has the right to make mistakes. I love you too much to keep trying to save you and make sure everything goes all right."
ROBERT: *(stunned)* "Well . . . that's okay, Mom."

2. All of us have the inalienable right to protest— Just as griping about taxes makes us feel better about having to pay them, teens often feel more understood when their parents accept their protests. There is then no reason for them to up the ante to disrespect. But, in cases of extreme disrespect, it may be best to ask your teen to come back later. A wise parent says, "I have trouble listening to this," rather than, "Don't talk that way!"

3. Back talk may be a symptom of a deeper problem— When back talk is one of several other symptoms, including poor school behavior or irresponsibility, a different approach may be necessary. Instead of allowing more freedom with consequences, parental structure may need to be tightened and consequences imposed rather than being allowed to occur naturally. Professional help is in order when teen problems are deeper than back talk and failure in school.

♥

Teens talk back when we threaten their independence

16

Friends

THERE IS NOTHING MORE SADDENING TO A PARENT THAN HEARING, "Nobody likes me," or "I don't have any friends." And, most parents feel unsure about what to do when this sort of thing happens.

What does research say about childhood friendships? Studies have shown that children unable to build and maintain friendships often have serious mental health problems as adults.

Do not panic if your child does not have a lot of close friends! Everyone is different. Some of us need and have a lot of friends. Some of us need, and have, just one or two.

What is important is that a child has at least one same-age friend who gives them the feeling of being important and valued.

When should a parent be concerned? If a child has no friends, this is a problem. Also, if a child's only friends are much older or much younger than the child, this is a concern. When children play only with much younger children, it's a sign that the child lacks the skills or maturity to develop relationships with kids his or her own age. When friends are much older, the child may be learning things he or she shouldn't—and may be being harmed by kids who enjoy the control they get from manipulating a younger child.

What can a parent do if their child is having problems making friends his or her own age? The first step is trying to understand why the problem exists. There are two general reasons kids have problems making friends. First, the child may simply lack the skills necessary for building friendships. What are these skills? Children

need to know how to smile. They need to know how to introduce themselves in a friendly way. They need to know how to share. They need to know how to compliment others. They need to know how to joke and be silly when it's appropriate. The best way to teach these skills is modeling them and having brief discussions with your children about their importance.

The second general reason children have trouble making and keeping friends has more to do with how the child feels about himself, and the world. When a child feels poorly about self, angry at the world, depressed, anxious, or fearful, it's obviously quite difficult for them to learn and use friendship skills. What's the solution here? Children who hurt in this way need someone who can listen and care. They also need someone with the training and expertise necessary for helping them overcome these emotional obstacles. If your child is too angry, anxious, or depressed to make friends, please take the time to consult with a qualified mental health professional.

❤

Childhood friendships are essential for a happy, healthy life!

17

Chores

CHORES ARE AN IMPORTANT PART OF A CHILD'S LIFE. They provide the foundation upon which responsibility and high self-esteem are built. Chores need not, indeed, should not be a cause of parent/child friction.

GUIDELINE 1:

When children are small, enjoy doing things together—
When children are small they like to "copy" and "model" their parents. When they are small they say, "Let me do it." (Oh, wouldn't it be a joy if they said that at 10!) Little ones like to stir around in the dishwater as the parent does the dishes. They like to dress up just like their parents. They like to push around their Fisher-Price lawnmower as if really cutting the grass. So, during the toddler years, it is the wise parent who communicates the following messages:

• "Hey, do I ever like getting my job done around the house. It's fun for me!"
• "Wow, do I ever enjoy doing things with you!"
• "Don't we have fun together!"

GUIDELINE 2:

Base chores on the maturity of your child— I say "maturity" because maturity level may not always reflect the child's actual age. Generally, however, through kindergarten, the child is no real help with most tasks. During the preschool and kindergarten years, the correct attitude about chores is built mainly by parents modeling and "working" with the child. Preschool and kindergarten children may be expected to clean up messes they make, help clean up their rooms, and make their beds (even if only in a sloppy sort of way).

By third grade and throughout the rest of the elementary school years, most children can take care of the dishes and clean a few of the family rooms once a week. Other jobs they can handle include cleaning the garage, cleaning the car—inside and out, taking out the trash, and cleaning ovens and dirty windows.

GUIDELINE 3:
The secret of happiness with your child around chores is to use consequences without anger— Children do not need to be rewarded for finishing a job. However, compliments and happiness are important. All of us like to hear more excitement about things done right than things done wrong! All of us need positive comments and interactions with others. If parents convey more emotion about jobs done poorly than jobs done well, you can bet jobs will continue to be done poorly.

I do not recommend tying allowance to chores. This is not the way the real world works. Parents don't get paid for fixing dinner or going shopping. It's expected as part of their contribution to the family unit.

The rub comes in applying appropriate consequences, without anger, when jobs have been done poorly or have not been completed. Let's look at this example:

A new parent, trying to be a good parent, once asked a mother why she was able to do a better job of raising eight children than most people did with one. The mother thought for a while and finally said, "Well, I really don't know. All I can say is, if the eggs aren't gathered, nobody has breakfast."

That's it! How simple. It's just like the real world. First do your job, then you can eat! This young parent used the idea. As her children grew into adulthood, she always let them know that she would like the job done by the time they ate their next meal. They could take their time. No rush. But she found the job was always done by dinnertime.

❤

Chores are the foundation of responsibility and self-esteem

18

Fighting and Bickering

CHILDHOOD FIGHTS. They can be tough on parents as well as on children. Luckily, there are guidelines on how fights should be handled most of the time.

GUIDELINE 1:
Protect if life and limb are in danger—otherwise expect the children to handle it— The first guideline is the toughest. When we hear children fighting, we naturally want to intervene. In some cases, if we are teachers, we have a legal responsibility to intervene whether or not it is necessary. However, if possible, it's best to put the problem on the children. When one child tattles on another, it's best to say, "Why are you telling me?" Or, on seeing a fight, sometimes it works to say, dryly, "You two ought to form a committee" or, "Please settle it somewhere else where I won't see it or hear it."

GUIDELINE 2:
Help children to problem solve their fights— Children need help in identifying their feelings. Were they feeling mad, sad, frustrated, or left out? After identifying their feelings, they can then identify different ways to handle them. We can use modeling at this point: "If I hit Mr. Jackson when I feel frustrated, I probably won't be as happy as I am handling it in another way. How do you think you could handle your problem in another way?"

GUIDELINE 3:
"Use "I-messages"— When we are around youngsters who fight, they must understand we are going to take care of ourselves rather than try and take care of them. Then, if we do need to ask the children

to leave or quit playing together, they are not resentful. They *would* be resentful if they thought we were doing it for their own good. If we do it for *our* good, they accept it. It's almost magic. Adults giving "I-messages" might say: "Fights make me nervous," or "Hey, have you two had your rabies shots?" or "Hey, guys, this stuff hassles my eyeballs." I want to stress here the importance of humor.

GUIDELINE 4:

Give consequences only if a difficult child has trouble dealing with a contract for no fights— A therapist tells the story of Jake who came to the office with his professional foster parent. Jake had been a terror when he arrived in the foster care program three weeks earlier. Now his fighting had almost stopped. When the therapist asked Jake about this, he said, "Well, I hate doing the chores. When I fight, my mom says it drains energy from the family. But when I scrub the walls, it puts energy back into the family." Jake, I might note, said this without any anger toward his foster parents. As he told this, he looked up at his mother, with the dawning of love, and smiled.

These consequences were meted out to *take care of the mother*, not to take care of Jake. Further, his mother did not have to tell Jake what to do. She didn't have to say, "Stop fighting!" Such orders seldom work on children like Jake. Instead, his wonderful parents could see what was happening, stop Jake, and say in a loving way, "Jake, I feel an energy drain coming." Jake changed quickly!

❤

Let the Children Solve the Problem—
Avoid Being Used As a Judge or Referee

19

Reasoning with Children

"I DON'T KNOW WHAT'S WRONG WITH THOSE KIDS. They never listen to a thing I tell them. I might as well be talking to the wall for all they care!"

Does this sound familiar? How do we get kids to listen and benefit from our experience and knowledge? Maybe it's just asking too much. Or is it?

We could blame this problem on the belief that youngsters are just headstrong and determined to learn the hard way. It's also possible that many parents try to reason with their children at the wrong time. This greatly reduces their chances for success.

We've all watched parents give their children a "good talking to" with little or no positive results. This is unfortunate because the adult not only had good intentions but good advice to share. The only trouble was that the child was not in an emotional state that would allow listening and use of the adult's wisdom.

The words we use with our kids during emotional times are wasted— They are either never heard or are turned against us. We all have difficulty listening during emotional times. It's natural, at times like these, to focus most of our thoughts upon the emotions rather than the words being spoken. As a result, we remember the other person's anger better than we remember the words.

A child at the dinner table who is not eating and who is complaining about the food provides a good example. Reminders in this case seem to do little good.

One parent might handle it by using angry-sounding words like, "What's wrong with you? Don't you come to the table with that attitude. You quit that complaining," or "I'll really give you something to complain

about!" My guess here is that the child is thinking a lot about the adult's anger and little about the wisdom of eating a good meal.

Use soft words with actions— Another parent might replace these angry words with soft words and action: "I'll be picking up the food and dishes in five minutes. I hope by then you will have eaten all you need to hold you until breakfast." Nothing is said if the youngster does not eat. The words are saved for a time when the child will be better able to listen.

It is obvious that the child will be hungry later and say, "I'm hungry. What can I have?"

This wise parent knows that the youngster will learn more when few words are used: "I bet you are. That's what happens to me when I miss my dinner. I bet you'll be anxious for breakfast. Don't worry. We'll cook a good one."

This parent chose to save the words for a time when the child was in the *thinking state* rather than in the *emotional state*. The best time for reason is when both the child and the adult are happy. This is the time when the best thinking and learning can take place.

❤

Save the Words for Happy Times

20

Trying on New Hats— Why Teens Rebel!

SOME TEENAGERS SEEM TO CHANGE THEIR VALUES WEEKLY AND EVEN DAILY. If they believe what their parents believe, it means they are not individuals! Some teens have radar that picks up which values are most important to us, and then they abandon those values. Wise parents recognize that it's normal for adolescents to "try on new hats" (new values.) They also know this rebellion is not permanent.

The following are ways to "release" your teen from certain values and prevent them from becoming permanent:

1. Don't criticize what your teen says— When parents criticize, teens feel they must clamp on to certain values for dear life to prove their individuality!

2. You can't force change— The best way to guarantee someone does not change is to order them to change! With teens, this only makes them intensify their behavior to prove they're OK. Then we may have locked them into the value—permanently.

3. Practice saying "Thanks for sharing"— When his son told him that nothing was wrong with adultery, a wise father responded with, "Thanks for sharing that. I wondered how teenagers saw that issue." He then went on to say, "That sure wouldn't work for me, but I can understand how a teenager could see it that way."

When a parent simply says, "Thanks for sharing that," a teen has no need to hang on to the value. They can eventually discard it and move on!

4. Don't tell teens they are wrong— The fastest way to make an enemy is to tell someone they are wrong. It works every time! A wise salesman once said, "You can't make someone mad and sell them something at the same time!" Parents may wonder why they can't "sell" their teens on their beliefs or values.

The answer lies in the way parents communicate with their children when they talk about values the two don't share. Parents who listen, without anger, cause teens to talk themselves out of the value.

5. It's OK for teens to make mistakes— Einstein said the way to become a genius is to make lots of mistakes and learn from them in a short period of time. Our children need more practice experiencing the consequences of their mistakes and actions and then experiencing our empathy—rather than our anger.

As much as we would like to prevent our teens from making the same mistakes we made growing up, it never works. They simply say, "Let me make my own mistakes!"

It helps to look back and remember how much we learned in life from those valuable mistakes we were allowed to make.

❤

It's OK for teens to make mistakes

Chapter Three

21

Arguing

YOUNG PEOPLE NEED TO KNOW their parents mean it when they set limits. Parents need to know that there are ways to say "no" without waging a major battle.

I wish your children would thank you for having the strength to set limits. But children have never been known to say, "Thanks, Dad, I feel a lot more secure now that I know you mean what you say. Thanks for loving me enough to set these limits." Instead, they may pout, complain, stomp around, run to their rooms, whine, or talk back. This often leaves the adult angry and confused.

Why are children so testy when we give them limits that help build their sense of security and self-confidence? Children need to test limits just to make sure they are firm. Each youngster seems to have his or her own special testing routine. Some use anger, some use guilt, some are sneaky, while others use forgetting to test your resolve.

It helps parents to remember that kids hear the word "no" far too often. It seems to be a call to arms, a fighting word. A child often wages war against "no" in a very subtle way—by trying to get the parent to do all the thinking while he or she stands back and criticizes.

You can turn the tables on children by forcing them to do most of the thinking. *Just replace "no" by saying "yes" to something other than the child's explicit request/demand.* Use "thinking words" instead of "fighting words." For example:

Fighting words: "No, you can't go out to play. You need to practice your lessons."

Thinking words: "Yes, you may go out to play as soon as you practice your lessons."

Most youngsters will try to argue when faced with "thinking words." However, since you started the conversation with "yes" instead of "no," you shouldn't feel guilty or explain or justify anything. State-of-the-art arguing is now in your hands. *No matter what your child says, simply agree that it is probably true. Then add the word* "and." *Follow this by repeating your first assertion.*

Compare these two approaches:

TEEN: I need to use the car to go skiing.
DAD: You can't use the car until you pay your gasoline bill.
TEEN: But, Dad, I promised my friends.
DAD: Why don't you make them drive?
TEEN: But you don't like the way they drive!

Here's how Dad could guide the teen to do all the thinking:

TEEN: I need to use the car to go skiing.
DAD: Feel free to use it as soon as your gasoline bill is paid.
TEEN: But, Dad, I promised my friends.
DAD: I'm sure that's true ... and ... feel free to use it as soon as you pay the bill.
TEEN: But I have to buy the lift ticket.
DAD: I bet that's true too ... and ... feel free to use the car as soon as you pay ...
TEEN: I know! Don't say it again.

Easy-to-learn tools like the above example can be used to eliminate fights with your children.

❤

*There is nothing wrong with a child
that a little arguing won't make worse*

22

The Gift of Struggle

ARE WE STEALING FROM OUR CHILDREN? Despite our best intentions, we may be robbing them of the opportunity to struggle, leaving them vulnerable to underachievement and suicide.

Schools today face an epidemic of underachievers, yet these children believe with all their hearts that they are incapable of doing the work asked of them. They say school is boring, irrelevant, or too hard. They may seem confused, under constant stress, or incapable of doing more.

Well-meaning friends may suggest that parents be more understanding, more supportive, or more helpful with studies. Sometimes these tips are helpful, but often they are the worst possible advice.

Mom and Dad "To-the-Rescue"

These same children may have similar problems when it comes to doing tasks at home. They have learned at an early age that adults will rescue them when the going gets tough. Children quickly become addicted to adult help and begin to believe the adults' unstated message that they can succeed only with assistance.

Underachievers often have parents who had to struggle when they were children. They grew up to say, "I don't want my kids to struggle like I did. They deserve better." Their children live in a home where struggle is an enemy rather than an opportunity.

The problem was less severe years ago. Parents preoccupied with the Depression, World War II, and scratching out a living, gave their kids tasks that forced them to help the family. Struggling at home prepared children to struggle at school.

Today's underachievers believe failure is too painful. Yet recent studies demonstrate children denied the opportunity to struggle during their early years are at high risk for suicide. They are unable to see themselves solving problems.

Solutions

The answer is to give children responsibilities. Children need jobs to do around the house, and they need parents who consider this a top priority. The most effective way to do this is to say to your children, "There's no hurry on the chores. I just want them done before your next meal." Missing a meal is momentarily unpleasant, but avoiding a struggle hurts self-concept in the long run.

I was recently asked if chores should be assigned to a teenager who has a lot of studying, many school responsibilities, and a part-time job. Teenagers become experts at believing they have more important things to do than chores. They even decide that studying is more important. My answer was, "Absolutely! Chores come first. Say to your youngster, "I hope you get your chores done fast enough so the rest of your activities won't suffer."

Sylvia B. Rimm, Ph.D., author of the *Underachievement Syndrome,* says many learning problems at school are cured when children are given chores at home. One of her 12 tips for helping underachievers: "Children feel more tension when they are worrying about their work than when they are doing their work."

❤

Struggle Produces S-T-R-E-T-C-H-I-N-G AND GROWING

23

Parents vs. Grandparents Who Bosses the Kids?

"How COULD YOU LET DREW DO THAT?" asks the critical grandparent, making the grown parent feel like a young child again. Before we blast on our parents or give in, we might want to consider this observation from psychologists: the way we treat our own parents is the way our children will tend to treat us.

There are techniques for coping with overly critical or intrusive grandparents. To begin with, most of us need to remind ourselves that we may go through life never being totally accepted by our parents, especially if they have always been very critical with us. All the energy spent searching for their acceptance may only end in frustration. Once we realize that we cannot make our parents accept us as parents of their grandchildren, we can use our energy on the techniques that do foster healthy relationships.

"Do's" that work— These techniques are similar to guidelines for handling children:
• Be assertive
• Take care of yourself in a loving way
• Concentrate on problem solving rather than on frustration and anger
• Provide consequences if necessary

Looking for a positive way to handle a grandparent's critical statement is better than "reacting" to that statement. For instance, a parent might say to his/her own parents, "Dad and Mom, before you comment or talk to me about how I raise the children, I hope you

will first ask me in a loving way why I am handling things the way I do. Does this sound reasonable to you?"

Bottom-line expectations— Sometimes we need to clarify our bottom-line expectations. One request parents might make of grandparents is that they refrain from making negative comments on parenting techniques in front of the children. Another bottom-line request might be that the grandparents refrain from disciplining the children without the parents' permission. Grandparents, too, have rights. If the children are acting like hellions, grandparents have a right to ask their children to handle it, or even ask the entire tribe to leave.

Why we interact— Sometimes parents need to say, "Mom and Dad, some of the reasons people get together are (1) to have fun, (2) to get something accomplished, or (3) out of a sense of obligation or guilt. I'm wondering if you see our times together as fun. If not, what do you see as the answer? I want you to know that I'm unwilling for us to relate purely out of a sense of obligation or guilt. How can we get together to have fun rather than argue like this?"

As we look at the conflict, it might be important, following an accusation or a cutting comment from our parents, to ask, "Is there any answer or response that I could give you right now that would really make you happy? I love you too much to see us at odds like this."

Let us also remember that the techniques we use with our children today may be very different than those used by our parents to raise us. A kind and thoughtful act is to explain to our parents why we choose to raise our children the way we do.

❤

Setting Bottom-Line Requests with Grandparents
Can Reduce Family Stress

24

Open Talk about Sex

IT IS A RARE PARENT WHO DOESN'T WORRY about the sexual activities of their teenager. Their concerns are understandable in light of the fact that nearly all boys and the majority of girls have been sexually active before graduation from high school. Many, unfortunately, are sexually active in junior high.

The following points are provided to give parents insight into the often-sensitive subject of teenage sex:

1. Prohibitions will not stop a teen from having sex. Sex is addictive.

2. Parents often display hypocrisy. While worrying about their children, they may not be handling their own sexual lives in an open or conventional manner.

3. Prohibiting adolescent sexuality is not the issue. The challenge is to keep lines of communication open between parents and teens.

A father's worry about his daughter's sexual activities illustrates these points. In his desperation, he insisted on dropping her off at school every morning and picking her up every evening. Naturally, she became pregnant during the noon hour!

Finding the Right Words

Parents who enjoy good relationships with their teens and who are open about sex may find themselves faced with awkward questions like, "When did you first have sex?"

The following rule applies when parents are asked personal questions about their own sexual lives:

Parents reserve the right to their own privacy. Therefore, they answer their teens in general terms and keep specifics to themselves.

When teens ask why they should not have sex, parents are often at a loss for words, except to say, "Don't." A better response is the one this mother provides in a loving and non-accusatory manner:

"Honey, I want you to enjoy and love sex your whole life. If you have early experiences you feel bad about, they might affect the relationship you have later with your husband. That's why I hope you wait—until you are certain you want to be intimate, have seen a doctor about contraceptives, and feel really right about it."

Discussion Is Not Approval

Parents often worry that talking to their children about contraceptives is perceived as giving them approval to have sex. But providing teens with information or our thoughts on sex does not mean we approve of premarital or promiscuous behavior.

Today's teens need facts—on venereal disease, AIDS, pregnancy, and contraceptives. And parents can provide this information in a loving and matter-of-fact manner. For parents unsure of the facts, a wide range of books and articles are available concerning the risks of casual sex.

By being loving, accepting, and nonjudgmental, we can ensure our children have all the facts they need regarding the joys and dangers of sexual behavior.

♥

*Discussing Sex with Your Teen
Is Not an Endorsement for Promiscuity*

25

Hassles: What You Get Is Your Own Quota

ALL OF US HAVE DIFFERENT "HASSLE QUOTAS." This is a measure of what we expect to put up with in life. A "hassle quota" affects what we expect from our spouses and what we expect from our children. The higher our hassle quota, the more we expect negative behavior.

For instance, the hassle quota differs for each of two young mothers with 15-month-old infants. Both have infants who have tried crying at night.

Mom Number One, troubled by a high hassle quota, says, "What can you do? You just can't leave her in her bed crying for half an hour. I'm just getting no sleep at night!" Unconsciously this mother is saying, "Oh, what a hassle life is!"

Mom Number Two, who enjoys a low hassle quota, says of her infant, "Well, I found if I don't get up when Katherine cries, she sleeps through the night." This mom has no expectation that life will be a constant hassle.

The parent with a high hassle quota will move anything out of an infant's reach that might hassle their home. That same parent will become involved in a child's fight—anticipating the worst from the child while also depriving the child of learning experiences. The hassle quota has a powerful but unseen influence on everyone!

Often one hassle leads to another causing the "Hassle Cycle." People with a high hassle quota always think that things are "done" to them and many times find themselves in the "Hassle Cycle." Their hassled state makes it difficult to make good decisions about the ownership of problems.

For example, I saw a very hassled mother screaming at a crying child, "Don't you do that to me!" In reality, the child was only crying because she was very tired. This poor mother is now owning the hassle of others.

Had this mother said to herself, "That's sad for my child to be so tired and crying," she might have saved herself from entering the "Hassle Cycle."

In summary, everyone reading this article has expectations about hassles. The more hassles we expect, the lower our expectations of others. Individuals with a high hassle quota expect their children to be hassles at school and at home. They say, "Isn't that the way things are?" Unfortunately, for them, the answer is "yes."

❤

Stay out of the Hassle Cycle by Deciding
Who Really Owns the Problem

26

Handling Friends

IF YOU'RE UNHAPPY ABOUT THE COMPANY your son or daughter keeps, the secret is an open mind. In the long run, if we maintain a strong and loving relationship with our children, they will generally choose friends we approve of and some we even genuinely like!

Preserve Your Relationship

Our relationship with our teens has a major effect on the friends they choose. Love and open lines of communication are by far the best ways to ensure our children will make wise and reasonable choices.

For a short period of time, it is both normal and natural for a young person in the early teen years to seek friends whose values seem to be the very opposite of our own!

But sadly, some parents overreact by trying—usually without success—to control the friends their teenagers prefer to "hang out" with. Not only does this jeopardize the parent/teen relationship, it's also a waste of time.

No Criticizing

As parents, we should never criticize or judge people we don't know—and that includes our teen's friends. Our teenagers will eventually just ignore our thoughts and opinions. It's also well worth our time to get to know their friends and accept them as much as we possibly can. Sometimes, we end up pleasantly surprised and wonder why we were so concerned in the first place!

Our children often find good in others that we simply can't see—until it's too late. One mother laments, "To think I wouldn't let my

daughter date a boy in high school that later became a Rhodes scholar. How was I to know he'd turn out so great!"

Nonjudgmental Communication

Although it's unwise to criticize our teenager's friends, we certainly have the right to express our concerns. Our opinions should only be given in a loving and nonjudgmental manner. Example:

Joan's mother remains accepting and trusting—even when inside, she'd prefer that her daughter stay home rather than go out with friends she disapproves of. "Joan," she says, "I sure hope that some of you manages to rub off on Cindy and Jan. Sometimes I think those kids need you and are lucky to have you around. Maybe you're a good influence on them. Have a good time tonight, honey."

Parents might also say, in a gentle way, that they would probably choose a different type of person for their own friend, but then acknowledge that everyone has to make their own decisions in life.

Last Resort

We know it is generally useless to try to control who our teens are with when they're away from home. As a last resort, however, it is within reason for a parent to forbid certain friends of their teens to visit their home. This decision should only be made when less severe options have been tried—since such harsh action can harm the relationship a parent has built with their son or daughter.

❤

*A Loving Parent/Teen Relationship Is the Best Insurance
That Our Teens Will Choose the Right Friends*

27

Reducing Family Stress

STRESS IN FAMILIES TENDS TO COME from two sources: communication problems or outright personality problems.

Fortunately, communication problems lie at the root of a great deal of family stress. These problems are easier to handle than personality problems, since communication is usually enhanced by learning a few basic tools. Most of us are "easy to educate," if willing.

Here are two questions to determine whether there is a personality or a communication problem. First, ask yourself if the stressed-out person would be hard to live with no matter what stress he or she encountered. Second, ask if he or she would be stressed-out no matter who he or she lived with.

If the answers are, "yes," then the individual needs help. If the stressed individual says "yes" to therapy or outside counseling, personality problems can often be addressed. However, if the individual says "no" it becomes *our* problem and *we* need help. The self-help groups, such as twelve-step programs like Al-Anon, emphasize how to take care of ourselves when living with negative and difficult partners.

Tips to try: When the problem is communication, the use of "I-messages" often helps. "I-messages" tell the other person where I stand rather than where they need to go! "I-messages" tend to be assertive rather than aggressive.

Instead of telling children, "Be quiet," a wise parent might say, "I would appreciate less noise, please…. Thank you," in a tone of voice that imparts love and assumes compliance. Using an "I-message," a spouse might say, "Dear, it would help me if you left your problems at work. I know that's hard, but when you bring problems

home, I feel lots of stress." Such a statement is less likely to result in friction than if we shout, "Hey, don't take your work problems out on me!"

Sense of humor: Studies at the Cline/Fay Institute in Colorado show that a sense of humor, by itself, tends to help many individuals cope with stressful situations.

My problem or theirs?: Individuals who communicate well tend to separate problems into "mine" and "the other guy's." We can always *care* about other people's problems, but we need to *work* on our own.

When we help another person without their permission, they usually end up resentful rather than grateful. It is best to react to our children's problems with, "Gee honey, I hope you figure it out." However, if we face our children's problems with the attitude, "Now what can I do?" their response is likely to be, " I don't know, but I hope you figure it out, Mom and Dad!"

Life throws us waves of stressful situations along with troughs of peaceful periods. To cope with the stress, we need to thoughtfully look at our own family patterns and communication issues in a preventive way. This analysis is best done when we're in one of those peaceful times.

❤

Separating "your problems" from "my problems" helps us both

28

Meaning Business

MEANING BUSINESS DOES NOT MEAN SHOUTING OR BEING MEAN. Yet count-less parents at shopping centers and fast food restaurants shout to their kids, "No, you can't have that, and I *mean* it!" Recently, I heard a mother pleading, "Joycie, please, come on. How many times do I have to tell you!"

Summary of Rules for Meaning Business:

1. Avoid saving a child from the naturally occurring consequences of his or her mistakes. This does not mean that we don't care! We care, we simply do not rescue. We say, "How sad you have to stay after school," rather than, "Get your homework done!" There is an exception to this rule. If the child is doing something that is likely to cause danger to life and limb, parents must stop it.

2. Parents who mean business do not give warnings. For instance, if the children are misbehaving, wise parents might say, "Will you guys please take it outside"—rather than saying—"If you continue to stuff noodles up your nose I'm going to have to ask you to leave the table."

3. Important talk means *quiet* talk. Never, but never, try to out-shout a child. Quiet parent talk might be, "I'm sorry you won't be going with us" or "I was planning to leave with you at eight o'clock, but now I'm simply planning to leave at eight o'clock." Kids learn at a very young age, "Gee, they're talking soft! I'd better listen."

4. Parents who mean business are slow to tell their children what to do but may often comment on their own actions. For instance: "My tendency is to buy more for people in stores when they don't nag"

or, "I'll be eating dinner tonight with people I'm happy with—that may or may not include you."

In short, the rules for "meaning business" with our children are the same rules that are applied to us by businesses in our community. Our banker tends to talk quietly to us. He does not protect us from consequences—if we don't repay the loan, the car is simply repossessed! The real world that our children are entering is a no-nonsense, low-key, no-shouting place with consistent consequences. Parents do well to offer loving concern instead of automatic bail-outs when things go wrong.

❤

Loving Concern Instead of Shouting Matches and Automatic Bail-Outs Work Best When Things Go Wrong

29

When Teens Won't Talk

IF YOU'RE WORRIED BECAUSE YOUR TEEN WON'T TALK, take heart! There is probably more reason to worry about a teen who shares everything with you. But many parents, accustomed to talkative youngsters, blame themselves when their children both grow up and clam up!

It is absolutely normal for young people to withhold information from adults. Why? The following are a few reasons:

Teens don't feel safe sharing certain things with their parents— We have a natural tendency to become angry and upset when our teens tell us certain things. It's a rare and wise parent who says, "That's sad. I'm glad you shared that with me. How can I help you?"

Teens often think they are the only ones who have certain thoughts— Teens may not share embarrassing thoughts or problems with us because they think (often correctly) we won't be able to handle what they say.

Teens are seeking independence— A teen's thinking goes something like this: "If I tell my parents everything, that means I am not independent."

Teens sometimes lack the right words— Some adolescents don't talk because it may be difficult to find the words that match their feelings.

Teens are going through more changes than at any other time in life— The physical, emotional, and chemical changes taking place in a teen's body are intense. It's understandable why an adolescent behaves differently than the child who told you everything.

Help Your Teen Open Up

A few rules for parents can go a long way in helping our teens talk to us.

1. Don't interrogate— Parents who get the best results don't fire a lot of questions at their teenagers. Instead they say, "Let me tell you about my day!" Sometimes, their own enthusiasm rubs off.

2. Make it safe for your teen to talk— This means don't criticize. Don't tell your teen they're wrong—even when they are! A teen who is criticized will talk back or clam up even more. We need to show our teens we can handle what they say, without anger.

3. Don't try to force your teen to talk— A person's natural tendency is to keep quiet when someone tries to make them talk. Withholding information also makes some teens feel they are in control. Their silent message is, "You can't make me talk!" Keep in mind that teens will talk when they're ready and only when it's safe.

Normal and Natural

It's both normal and natural behavior for teens to keep information from adults. We're probably better off not knowing everything about them anyway!

❤

Make it safe for your teen to talk

30

Learning Life's Lessons

JOHN AND PAUL ARE YOUNG STUDENTS in elementary school, and they are neighbors. One night, after each of them misbehaved, their parents sent them to their rooms. For Paul, being sent to his room was a *punishment*. For John, it was a *consequence*. What's the difference? Both sets of parents did exactly the same thing.

The difference between consequences and punishment involves attitudes and feelings. Paul's parents led him to feel punished by sending him to his room with anger. His parents implied "Go up there and learn your lesson!" or, "Go up to your room and feel bad!" And you can bet that when Paul sat in his room, his head was filled with angry thoughts toward his parents. Worse yet, he was developing a poor self-image.

On the other hand, when John's parents said, "go to your room," they spoke without anger. Their implied message was: "We don't want to be around you, but you might enjoy yourself." They might have said, without sarcasm, "Go keep yourself happy company."

There are many examples of consequences. An elementary school child who had neglected his homework recently had to go to school early to get the work done; he had to take the junior high bus, which arrived at 6:30 a.m., instead of his regular 8:15 a.m. bus. Another child recently brought home a note from her teacher, who wrote, "No heavy thinking needed," meaning the child had a good day at school and could watch TV at home.

One child who regularly forgot his trumpet practice came home one day to find that the instrument had been sold. Recently a parent relying on consequences reminded her child that she was causing an

"energy drain" that could be replaced when the child did extra chores around the house. The child ruefully stated, "there's one thing I never want to do, and that's cause my mom an energy drain!"

So, we see that consequences are not designed to make a child feel sad, bad, inadequate, or wrong. Consequences are designed to make the parent feel better! In summary, the major differences between consequences and punishment include:

• Consequences make children think about their actions rather than how bad they feel about themselves or others.

• When experiencing consequences, children who get mad almost always get mad at themselves. (That's good!)

• Luckily, consequences often occur naturally. Parents do not always have to artfully impose them. Almost every action brings its own reward (or naturally occurring consequence).

Long-time school principal Jim Fay states it simply: "Punishment hurts the child from the outside in, while consequences help the child realistically hurt from the inside out!"

❤

CONSEQUENCES (Inside-Out Hurts) are more helpful than PUNISHMENTS (Outside-In Hurts)

Chapter Four

31

Getting a Headstart on Control

PARENTS WHO WANT TO GAIN CONTROL must first give away a little control. This means giving their children choices instead of demands whenever possible.

One of the most-often asked questions about choices is, "At what age can I start giving choices instead of orders?" Foster W. Cline, M.D., psychiatrist and cofounder of the Cline/Fay Institute in Golden, Colorado, tells us we can start choices about the same time our little ones can sit in a high chair and spit beets. Even if you no longer have a baby, Dr. Cline's advice may help you understand the need to offer choices.

A useful tip for parents to remember is that battles over food in the early years are usually fought again—in the subconscious mind— when the person becomes an adult. Therefore, it's unwise to have countless rules and battles about eating—whatever the child's age.

As soon as a baby spits food, the parent says, "Oh goody. Meal's over." The child is put down, and the food is put away. Notice there are few words and no anger.

Some people object, "That's too young. You can't reason with a child at that age." Dr. Cline says this objection assumes that the child is not as smart as the family dog. Isn't it interesting that we expect the dog, who has no language skills, to understand, but we want to wait until a child can talk before we think he or she can understand our actions?

Parents and teachers often try to reason with children instead of allowing them to learn from consequences. Have you ever seen anyone try to reason with the family German shepherd? "Now, Duke,

give me some eye contact so I can tell you what you just learned." We all know that would never work.

A child learns quickly that negative behavior doesn't pay. In the case of violating table rules, it takes only a few times for a child to learn the choices: eat nicely and have all you want, or act out and bring the meal to a halt.

To cap off this learning situation, the parent needs to hold his or her position that the next opportunity to eat will be the next mealtime. This must be done with empathy: "That's too bad, I get hungry too, if I don't eat enough when I have the chance. But don't worry, we'll be eating again soon."

❤

Let Consequences Not Words Teach a Child

32

Friends, Clothes, Looks, & Music

IT MAY BE HARD FOR PARENTS TO UNDERSTAND why the sounds blaring from the radio in their teen's bedroom are practically sacred to their son or daughter. But music, along with looks, friends, and clothes, are four things a parent should *never* criticize.

It's devastating to teens, who are seeking their own identities, when we criticize what's important to them. And, because a person's self-esteem is at an all-time low during the teen years, adolescents are even more sensitive to our opinions and the opinions of others.

It's more effective for parents to accept that clothes, looks, friends, and music are at the top of a teen's list of priorities. They're a major part of an adolescent's search for identity and individuality.

Friends

Teens often believe that spending too much time with their parents means they are neither independent nor individual. The more we find fault with their friends, the more they hang around them to prove their individuality.

Some teens dream about being wild, knowing deep down they never will be. To live out their fantasies, they sometimes choose friends their parents find objectionable. But that doesn't mean your teen will actually become wild—it just means they have found a "substitute" for their own dreams.

As parents, we should make every attempt to accept our teen's friends. We may even be pleasantly surprised by some of them!

Clothes and Looks

Clothes and looks are another way a teenager expresses the need to be different. Both can be healthy and nondestructive. If your teen is basically responsible, wearing an earring or a slightly weird hairstyle makes no difference!

The rule, again, is don't criticize. But if you're worried about what the relatives might think about your daughter's outfit, you might say something to her like this: "I'm a pretty reasonable parent, usually. Would it be OK for me to be just a little unreasonable this time? I mean I know what a great kid you are—but I'm not sure Aunt Betty will understand . . ." This kind of statement lets her daughter know what she wears reflects on her, not the parent.

Music

Parents who are overly critical about their teen's taste in music risk damaging the relationship they have built with their son or daughter. It's far more effective to acknowledge that teens and parents have different taste in music. There's certainly nothing wrong with asking your teen to keep the volume down or to use earphones.

You can't force your musical values onto your teen. The best way to get them to enjoy a different kind of music is to listen to it yourself and then talk about why you enjoy it instead of why *they* should.

❤

Friends, clothes, looks, and music are healthy ways
a teen expresses individuality!

33

Giving Control without Giving It Away

WE OFTEN HEAR HOW WISE IT IS TO GIVE OUR CHILDREN a certain amount of freedom and control over their lives. However, children who have more control than they know how to handle often act out in unbelievable ways to show us that they need limits. It's almost as if they are saying, "How bad do I have to act before you will control me?" This confuses parent and child alike. The child, having become addicted to power, demands more power while at the same time asking for parental control.

Children who start out with too much power force us to tighten the limits, and that makes them angry. Who wouldn't be mad? When control is taken away, children feel they are being robbed of something that is rightfully theirs.

Dr. Sylvia B. Rimm, psychologist, educator, and author, explains that we all compare the amount of control we have in a relationship to the control we *used* to have, not to how much we think we *should* have.

Dr. Rimm says loving parents use what she calls the "V" of love. The sides of the "V" stand for firm limits within which the child may make decisions and live with the consequences. The bottom point of the "V" represents birth, while the open top of the "V" represents the time when the child will leave home. Toddlers decide about such things as chocolate or white milk. Ten-year-olds are deciding how to spend their allowances and the 17-year-olds make decisions about almost all aspects of their lives. Unfortunately, the "V" is turned upside down in families where the child is treated almost like a

miniature adult right from birth. These youngsters become tyrants. We've all seen them hold their parents hostage to temper tantrums and pouting.

Children need the opportunity to make choices, but these choices should be within firm limits appropriate for their age. This is easier said than done. However, it helps to keep the "V" in mind, always leaving bigger decisions for the next year. Make sure there is more control available to the child this year than last.

Teachers are good resources regarding age-appropriate decisions for children. And remember, some of the greatest experts on parenting may be in your carpool or community. However, it is wiser to get advice from parents who have well-adjusted children than those whose youngsters are driving them crazy.

Make Sure There Is More Control Available to Your Child
This Year Than Last Year

34

Is It Normal for a Parent to Feel This Way?

IF YOU'RE TORMENTED BY SELF-DOUBT, constantly worried about how you're raising your teen, and often wonder why it's so difficult to be a parent, you're not alone!

Just as teens experience common feelings, so do the parents of teens. You might recognize yourself in the following descriptions:

Parents of Teens Feel Inadequate

Many of us experience self-doubt and seriously question our ability to parent. We ask, *"Am I too critical?"* or *"Am I strict enough?"*

Parents get down on themselves because what worked when their teens were youngsters no longer applies! While a certain amount of self-doubt is normal, we shouldn't go so far as to think we're "bad" parents.

Parents Feel a Loss of Control

When teenagers do things we can't stop, we feel a loss of control. It helps to ask, *"Were we meant to control our children?"* Teens, in particular, need free will. But many parents clamp down harder on their children as they grow older. The more determined we are to control, the more problems we have.

But the more we act as good advisors, asking questions in place of giving orders, the less resistance we see from teens.

Parents of Teens Feel Guilty

Guilt is a common feeling when our adolescents don't turn out the way we think they should. We spend a lot of time worrying about what others think of our ability as parents. Instead of worrying about what others think, go with the flow and do what you think is best!

Parents Have a Strong Desire to Enforce Tighter Rules

When teens start becoming more independent, our natural tendency is to make more rules. But as they grow older, there should be fewer, not more rules.

The last three years a teen is home should be like practice for the real world. And that means fewer rules and more negotiation on what both parents and teens can live with.

Parents Feel a Sense of Failure

So often we feel like we're failing. Do our kids help us feel this way? You bet they do! They let us know (and never let us forget) our weaknesses as parents. They are quick to remind us that all the other parents are doing a much better job!

But raising teens is a time of "goof and grow." We learn the hard way and make lots of mistakes. We shouldn't be so hard on ourselves—no matter what our teens tell us!

❤

Parents, Like Teens, Have Feelings of Doubt

35

"Smart Mouth" Can Be Cured

"What's wrong with her? No respect! Every time I turn around she's talking back." This complaint from a parent reminds me that concerns about kids who "talk back" come up often. Sassing is a frustrating problem.

Solving this problem usually requires a change of behavior for both child and adult. As an adult, I like to look at my own behavior first because it is something I can control. An effective way a parent can do this is to wait until the next time his or her youngster talks back and think, "What did I say a split second before the sassing happened?"

We often find that the child felt criticized and was reacting to the criticism. It is good to state reasonable expectations for a child, and it is very good to apply consequences with empathy for the child who does not meet those expectations. However, criticizing a youngster does not usually bring about any long-term behavior change. Instead, it breeds resentment and erodes self-confidence.

Once the parent has eliminated criticism, it's time to talk with the child. Brief discussion is useful when parents remember to discuss problems with children only during happy times. The purpose of this talk is to motivate the child to think about his or her actions and to learn new ways of talking so better understanding takes place.

The parent might begin by asking the child what he/she is angry about. It is absolutely necessary that the parent listen *without defending or judging*. The best reaction is to say, "Thanks for sharing."

A parent might also say, "Sandy, can you think of different ways you can answer me, so I'll know what you really want when you talk about it?"

To the usual response, "I don't know," the parent can respond, "Well, that's sad. But I bet you can come up with some new ideas. If not, let me know if you'd like some suggestions about how adults try to handle these things. Good luck!"

If the child has no idea what to say, the parent can ask if the child would like to hear some suggestions. Some words the child might use instead of sassing are: "That's embarrassing," or "I'm really angry," or "Can we talk about it?"

We often make progress with the problem of sassing when we eliminate criticism, help the youngster express his/her feelings, help the child find new words, and then provide practice.

❤

Children often talk back as a result of feeling criticized

36

Teen Pregnancy

WHEN A TEEN BECOMES PREGNANT, parents find themselves facing one of their worst fears. The stress surrounding an unmarried teenager's pregnancy can take its toll on even the strongest parents.

The parents of a pregnant teen are hurting deeply. Some feel they have failed or that they have not provided their daughter with enough love. They worry about the future of both their daughter and her unborn baby.

The teen is also hurting. She may feel intense guilt for letting her parents down or may be blaming herself for her irresponsible behavior. If the teen-parent relationship is poor, pregnancy may be one way of satisfying a need for love or "getting back" at her parents.

Counseling Is Critical

Even in this difficult situation, parents must remain calm and supportive. Parents must remain in a counselor role in order to help their daughter make some of the most important decisions of her life.

While a teen may discount her parents' wishes, she will often listen to others. Parents can help their daughter explore options, and her feelings about those options, through counseling available at family planning clinics or adoption agencies.

Don't Own the Problem

Today, thousands of "reluctant grandparents" are raising their teen's babies. If a daughter believes there is even the slightest possibility her parents might be talked into taking care of her baby, the parent could end up with her problem!

When parents are straightforward with their wishes, it narrows down the teen's options. Mom says to Julie, "I know this is one of the most difficult experiences of your life. Whatever your decision, we will support you. If you decide to keep the baby, know that we love you very much and will support that decision. However, please don't ask us to raise your child. That is definitely not an option for you."

Teens Who Keep Their Babies

Today, many teens are choosing to raise their babies. Many are from unhappy homes who have felt unloved most of their lives. To these girls, a child represents the answer to their dreams for fulfillment and love.

After the baby is born, reality sets in—babies don't give love, they demand it! Some young mothers become abusive. Others try to pawn their children off on their parents. Others may eventually choose adoption.

What about the Father?

Teenage fathers are also in a difficult position. Besides guilt, they may feel helpless. A father could be facing the support of a child for 18 years, if the mother decides to keep the baby. Parents need to make sure their teen sons fully understand the consequences of their actions.

Facing the Loss

Teens facing pregnancy also face many losses. Loss of innocence, loss of freedom, loss of trust.

❤

It's important that teens never lose a parent's love
and support over the pregnancy

37

Empathy Overpowers Anger

PARENTS WHO ARE STRONG ENOUGH to let youngsters experience the consequences of their actions also need to help them feel loved. Too often parents or teachers mete out consequences with anger. Missing empathy, the child feels no love and blames others for his/her own mistakes.

A parent recently told a nationally known educator and expert on child discipline that she needed help managing the art of empathy. Here is her story:

I keep getting mad when I give consequences. I get mad at my daughter, and then she gets mad at me.

I almost got to empathy last week. I was so close. My daughter didn't study her spelling words. I kept hearing your voice during your last lecture when you said, "These can be great opportunities. Don't blow them by nagging." So I didn't nag. I also heard your voice saying, "The school will provide the consequences. You can balance them with an equal amount of empathy."

She came home with a "D" on her test, and I did a great job of being sorry for her. I said, "Wow! It must really be embarrassing to get a "D". She got real quiet, thinking hard about what she had done. It was great!

Then I heard your voice in my head saying, "When you run out of things to say, transfer the problem to the youngster by asking a question." I said, "Wow! What are you going to do?" With the saddest little face, she said, "I don't know what I'm going to do."

I had her owning her own problem and thinking hard. And then ... I just had to do it. I don't know why, but I just blurted out, "And you're not going to that party on Friday!"

That did it! She started yelling, "What do you mean I'm not going to the party! It's not my fault I got a "D". You should see the words that teacher gives! She never gives us any time to study and ... it's just not fair."

Isn't it amazing? It only took one remark for me to change my daughter from a thinker to a fighter. So I'm back to work on empathy.

The educator, Jim Fay, of the Cline/Fay Institute in Golden, Colorado, told me recently that he hasn't seen this woman at his lectures for several months. He said he hopes she has mastered the art of giving equal amounts of consequences and empathy.

It helps to remember that using anger, threats, and lectures rarely works with children. Parents need to combine consequences with empathy. Those who deliver consequences in loving, firm tones find this far from easy. But it works.

❤

Empathy opens the mind for learning

38

Ten Guidelines for Handling Divorce

WHEN PARENTS DIVORCE, they may notice many problems with their children—defensiveness about touch, mood swings, problems in school, laziness, youngsters reverting to wetting their pants, hyperactivity in grade school children and back talk from teens.

Such behavior is often part of the normal grieving process and can be alleviated by following a few guidelines for divorced or divorcing parents:

GUIDELINE 1:
Expect children to handle the divorce as well as it is handled by the adults. Children follow our cues. If we're angry, they are. If we communicate, they do.

GUIDELINE 2:
Let the child know that the divorce is NOT the child's fault. A parent can say, "Michael, Dad and I decided we can't get along. We both still love you!"

GUIDELINE 3:
Be honest about your feelings. Parents need to tell their children, without details, how they feel about their ex-spouse and why. For example, "Dad and I had trouble agreeing on how we wanted to live in our marriage. I wanted him to be around a lot more, and he felt I limited his freedom." Notice it helps to provide the other parent's point of view.

GUIDELINE 4:
Understand why the child's acting out, but give consequences. Parents need to encourage the child to *express his/her feelings*.

If the parent lets the child be disrespectful, the child feels the adult is at fault and also feels guilty for misbehaving.

GUIDELINE 5:

Give the child someone outside the family to talk with, such as a school counselor, teacher, peer group, or family friend.

GUIDELINE 6:

Post-divorce counseling may help. When communication is poor after the divorce, counseling almost always helps, as long as both adults want to be civil.

GUIDELINE 7:

Remain available to the child without prying.

GUIDELINE 8:

Handle issues around visitation directly with your ex-spouse—not through your child.

GUIDELINE 9:

Children need "moms" and "dads." Encourage children to call stepparents "Mom" and "Dad." They won't forget their "real" parent.

GUIDELINE 10:

Parents must back the stepparent to the hilt on discipline.

❤

Children can be expected to handle a divorce
only as well as their parents do

39

Preparing Kids for the Teen World

THE WAY WE DISCIPLINE OUR CHILDREN in grade school determines the type of teenagers they become. In elementary school, both right and wrong ways of disciplining work! However, while inappropriate methods may work during a child's younger years, they fail to prepare a child for adolescence.

By following a few guidelines during the grade school years, parents can help their children glide through the teen years with minimal difficulty.

GUIDELINE 1:
Give your child as few rules as possible and as many as absolutely necessary— Generally, it's best to let the child make mistakes. Their consequences are usually far less severe in grade school than in high school.

GUIDELINE 2:
Let natural consequences occur— Grounding, anger, or lectures teach the child to resent the parent rather than learn from natural consequences. Wise parents, taking a cue from the airlines, say, "We're leaving at eight o'clock. If you are ready at that time, you may go with us."

GUIDELINE 3:
Wise parents impose consequences to take care of themselves— Effective consequences that parents impose include isolation of the child or having the child perform extra work around the house to

"pay the parents back" for family items they have abused. Wise parents say, "Why don't you take a walk around the block and cool off? We'll be happy to see your face again when there's a smile on it." When we take care of ourselves, children learn how to take care of themselves.

GUIDELINE 4:

Get the child's opinions and thoughts first— We ask with interest and without accusation.

GUIDELINE 5:

Parents should mean what they say, and say it only once— Often parents give warnings: "Now I mean it!" (which implies the parent usually *doesn't!*) Try instead, "Will you guys please take it outside now?" the kids may say, "What did we do?" A good response is, "Outside is the place to figure that out."

GUIDELINE 6:

Use spankings very sparingly— A rare swat on the rear by a parent may be appropriate when children are very small and learning basic obedience issues, such as "come," "sit," "no," "go," and "stay." However, regular spankings are generally ineffective.

To make these approaches more meaningful, discuss their pros and cons with your spouse or a friend before implementing any of them with your child.

❤

Positive Discipline During Grade School Helps Kids Glide through the Teen Years!

40

Learning Disorders— No Easy Answers

MANY CHILDREN, AS MANY AS TWO OUT OF TEN, are diagnosed as having a learning disorder, perceptual motor problem, and/or dyslexia. These common terms are used to describe a child who is normally intelligent but has problems in learning, usually academic learning.

Learning disorders rarely exist without behavioral problems and/or attitude problems at school. Many children may also have associated signs of definite neurologic "brain" dysfunction.

When a child has a "learning problem," the *specific* problem needs to be defined before a *specific* solution can be offered. Many learning problems can be *cured or helped,* while others need to be "coped with." Too often parents face needless agony, wheel-spinning, and financial cost when they try to fix a problem that will disappear with time, cannot be fixed, or is not the basic problem.

There are two ways of diagnosing learning problems. The first and *most important* is to obtain an accurate history, including birth or pregnancy problems, the age at which the child mastered such milestones as crawling, walking, and talking, and family history, such as whether parents or siblings had problems in school. Second, there are a number of tests that help clarify a learning disorder.

What to do about a problem is based on an accurate diagnosis, but there are some basics that apply to most learning disorders:

1. *No matter what the problem,* a child must feel good about him/herself while recognizing that he/she does have a problem in

learning. Wise parents and educators focus on *building a child's strengths* rather than *correcting weaknesses*. Strengths may be in nonacademic or extracurricular areas.

2. If a six-to-ten-year old, particularly a boy, was "slow" in milestone development, but now walks and talks normally and has a normal vocabulary but messy handwriting, problems in math, drawing, and spelling, he or she is likely to out grow most of the problems in the early teen years.

3. If a learning disorder is accompanied by Attention Deficit Hyperactive Disorder (ADHD), a physician may recommend medication. (ADHD is a whole different topic.)

4. If a child is to remain in the educational system, the size of the class, the behavior of the other children, and the ability of the teacher to respond to the child as a unique individual are the three factors most important to the child's success.

5. Tutoring, even by the best teacher, only helps when a child buys into the program.

❤

Focus on Building a Child's Strengths
Rather Than Correcting Weaknesses

Chapter Five

41

Building Cooperation with School People

THE IDEAL ROLE PARENTS PLAY in their child's school life centers around encouragement and good modeling. They leave the school discipline to the teachers and administrators and allow the child to handle his or her own school problems. However, there are times when things are not ideal and a parent must become involved in the school situation. This can be a difficult position. If it's not handled with tact, your child may feel unable to handle his/her own problems in the future.

Instead of storming into the teacher's room offering solutions, we need to collect information and think about the choices given.

Parents make three common mistakes when talking with teachers:

1. We tell the teacher what to do— When we say, "I want my kid out of that classroom," what we are really saying is, "You aren't smart enough to figure out what to do, so I've got to tell you."

2. We go into the school with threats— "If you won't help, I'm going to go to the principal." This creates even more problems than we had when we came in.

3. We muster an army of like-minded parents to assault the teacher en masse— Any victory in this sort of confrontation will be short-lived, for the teacher will fight for his or her life. A variation of this tactic is saying, "I'm not the only one who's upset with this situation; a lot of others are too."

Parents who get the best results with teachers use the magic word "describe." It's magic because when we use it we aren't judging: "I'd like to describe something that's happening, and then give you my interpretation of it."

When we've had our say, we can use some more magic words: "I'd like to get your thoughts on that." By saying this, we are telling the teacher that we have confidence that he or she can think for himself or herself. It is also a way of getting valuable and surprising information. For example, a child who is easy to work with at home one-on-one, may not respond the same way in a larger group. The teacher's reading of the situation is usually very helpful. We are able to get the teacher's best suggestions if we don't put the teacher on the defense.

Another approach is to ask, "What kind of options are available to solve a problem like this?" and then allow the teacher to do the thinking for a while. This shows the teacher that we are open to looking at more than one way of solving the problem. People who use this technique find that others are much more friendly and helpful.

In the event we get no satisfaction with the teacher, and want to kick the problem up the ladder, we should say, "Would you mind going with me to see if the princpal has any thoughts on this?" That's a whole lot better than saying, "If I don't get my way, I'm going to the principal."

Our chief mission in approaching a teacher is to discuss our child's problem and resolve it—to talk as well as listen, to suggest as well as take suggestions. Good common sense values of communication and respect for others are much more effective than commands and threats.

❤

"What kind of options are available to solve a problem like this?"
"I'd like to describe something that's happening."

42

When Are You Ever Going to Take Care of Your Stuff?

KIDS AND THEIR TOYS. We can be sitting in relative order one minute and, before we can turn a page in the evening paper, the room is trashed.

Unfortunately, some parents can't blame their kids for not picking up their toys. Our kids will do as we do. Parents who trash their room with mounds of clothes draping the chairs, usually raise children who want to act just like them.

In addition to caring for our own things, explaining how we feel when we pick things up sends a powerful message. Putting the dishes away, replacing the tools on their proper hooks, sweeping the sidewalks after mowing the grass—if we talk about it as we do it, and after we do it, our kids get the right message. A very effective father used to handle it this way, "Boy it feels good to finish this job, but I won't feel great until I get this mess picked up." As soon as he cleaned up, he would say, "Now I feel really great! Everything is in the right place." He said this out loud giving his children an opportunity to eavesdrop.

Until our kids are three or four years old, cleaning up their toys should be a community project. We put a toy away, then they put a toy away, then we put a toy away, and so on. As children grow older, their toys become *their* responsibility. What happens to their belongings is up to them.

One parent handled the issue like this:

PARENT: "Hey, Peter, there's a lot of your stuff laying around the

house today. It's getting in the way. Do you want to pick it up or would you rather I pick it up?"

PETER: "You pick it up."

PARENT: "Well, if you pick it up, you get to see it again. So you might want to rethink your decision on that. But you don't have to rush. If, by lunchtime, I still see the stuff out there, I'll know you decided to have me pick it up. If I see it's gone, then I'll know you decided to pick it up."

In the event the parent has to pick up the toys, the following discussion will probably result,

PETER: "Where's my stuff?"

PARENT: "Gone."

PETER: "Why?"

PARENT: "We agreed that if it was still laying around at lunchtime that I was supposed to pick it up."

The question then becomes, should we give the toys back? If our child is basically responsible, we say, "Every time you pick up all your toys by yourself without being told, you earn back one of those toys you lost today." With kids who have a hard-core problem with responsibility, they should know they are gradually saying "so long" to the toys we have to pick up. Don't be afraid of saying from time to time, "You know, I'm really worried about the way you're taking care of your stuff. I'm thinking maybe you need to be a little older before you have that responsibility. So, I'm going to take this toy until I don't have to worry about how well you're taking care of it. Don't worry, you'll get another shot at being responsible for it."

This is a great opportunity for the parent to solve the problem without anger or threats. It is also a great opportunity for the child to give this a lot of thought and have the chance to practice his/her responsibility.

❤

Explaining how we feel when we take care of our things, sends a powerful message to kids

Teen Telephone Use

The telephone is a wonderful parenting instrument! Like all instruments, it can be used appropriately by parents to help children learn responsibility, or it can be used inappropriately by parents and lead to numerous family hassles.

Discuss the Situation with Your Teen

If your teen is spending more time on the telephone than you would like, you might try discussing the situation.

"I know time on the phone with your friends is very important. Do you have any thoughts about how you can get that time and still balance out the rest of your life? I hope you can find a way to get your work done and still have time with your friends and some time with the family. What seems to make sense to you?" If your teen is looking for some options, be prepared with a menu of possible solutions:

• Some teens buy their own telephone line
• Some youngsters tell their friends to call during certain hours
• Some teens reserve dinnertime for family and don't talk on the phone during that time
• Some teens go live with their friends so they don't have this hassle
• Some teens exchange minutes on the phone for minutes of doing extra chores

Wise parents might discuss message taking with their teen:

"Robert, you can use the phone as much as you want. Whenever any of us are on the line, we will answer the other line when it clicks and take a telephone number for the other family member to call back. If you are on the phone and a telephone call

comes in for an adult who is present in the home, you will tell the caller you are on the phone right now, that you will get off the phone, and that you will immediately call the adult to the phone. Then, within two sentences, you will tell your friend good-bye, tell him you'll call back, and immediately call the adult to take the phone call. Is the picture clear?"

"Yeah," responds the teen, "It's clear, but that's unfair! How come you get to talk to people immediately and I have to wait?"

"That's because I pay the bills. Whoever pays the telephone bill gets to use the phone immediately. It's their phone. If the rule seems unfair to you, you can pay for another line, pay the monthly bill, and have your own phone in your room. (This is based on the supposition that any teen responsible enough to earn his/her own money and pay for a separate line and monthly bill is responsible enough to have his/her own phone in his/her own room. This is almost always true.)

Most children, considering the options, will agree they should immediately call their parents to the phone. In return, they get to use the phone, which is a real privilege.

Some adolescents, unfortunately, need to have the following additional conversation with their parents:

"Troy, if I have business associates or friends call, and they either get a busy signal or the phone rings, and there is no answer, and I find that it is a time when we were home and you were on the phone, how will the rules have to change to ensure that I always get my calls?"

"Well, I suppose you could ban me from the telephone so it would always ring through."

"What a good idea! Maybe we ought to all give that some thought. Do you think we will need that rule?"

"No, I guess not!"

"Thanks, Troy, you're a jewel!"

In a loving parent/child relationship, firmness and high expectations almost always ensure your adolescent will be pleasant, courteous, effective, and an always-present answering machine.

❤

A teen in the house means a free answering machine

44

Whining and Complaining

IT'S TEN O'CLOCK IN THE MORNING AND MIKEY WANTS A COOKIE. He knows he can't have one, but that doesn't stop him from asking.

"Mommy, I want a cookie," he whines, his little fist clutching a fold in Mom's skirt.

"Mikey, you know you can't have cookies between meals," Mom returns. "Now, run off and play."

"But Mommy, I want one," Mikey continues.

"You can have one at lunchtime. Now, off you go."

"Mommy, I don't want to wait. I want one now."

"Well, you can't have one."

And then it happens. There's something about parents who tolerate whining from their kids: eventually the parents whine back. "Will you stop that whin-n-n-ning?" Mom says. "I hate it when you whine like that."

No wonder Mikey whines like he does. He has a good teacher. The fact is, parents who spend a lot of time pleading with their children, raise kids who are experts at pleading themselves.

Oftentimes, just to get rid of that sing-songey record of complaint, we give up the battle and grudgingly fork over the cookie or whatever our child has been whining for. The message the child gets is that whining works.

The secret of handling whiney behavior is similar to that of dealing with disrespect. We must make it known to our child that he or she will get no results until the tone of voice changes.

Some effective school teachers fight whiney behavior with multiple-choice questions. "Do you suppose I'll be able to understand

you better when you're whining, or not whining? Why don't you think about that. Come back when you've decided."

We can do the same. Saying "When your voice sounds like mine, I'll be glad to talk with you," addresses the real problem with whining, which is the tone of voice the child uses. Whether or not Mikey can have a cookie will be discussed later, after the syrupy pleading stops.

Kids are nothing if not persistent. Sometimes saying "I won't listen to you while you're whining," gives them the emotional feedback they're looking for and encourages them to keep on.

If we aren't getting results by asking them to leave, or if we find ourselves drawn into a discussion about it, then we can win the battle by ignoring the whining altogether. It is best, however, to explain this method before employing it. Sit the child down, when emotions are calm, and say, "Mikey, if we ever act like we don't hear you, it's not because we don't *want* to hear you. We'll respond when we hear you talk in the same tone of voice we talk in."

Parents have the best luck when they rehearse their reaction to whining until they hear themselves thinking, "I can't wait for little Jeff to whine. I hope he does it today so I can practice my new techniques. Come on kid, make my day!"

❤

Address the real problem with whining—
the tone of voice used

45

It's OK to Catch Your Teen Doing Something Right

IT MAY COME AS A SURPRISE FOR SOME PARENTS to learn that most teens are suffering from a strong case of self-doubt. In fact, a person's self-concept is usually lower during the teen years than at any other time in life.

Self-doubt in teens is normal. It usually stems from the enormous social, emotional, physical, and hormonal upheaval they are experiencing. Over a period of time, parents can help turn these feelings of self-doubt into healthy feelings of self-worth.

We Should Not Only See Our Teens but Hear Them

Telling teens they are good won't help them build self-confidence. They *will always* discount what we say.

It's better to find your teen doing something right. Then say, "I noticed how good you're getting with the computer," or "I've noticed you've really improved at softball."

Then, listen to your teen. Ask why he or she thinks things are turning out so well. When teens actually say what they did to achieve success, it helps them build a stronger self-image.

Whenever possible, look at your teen's school, chores, and other activities. Say, "You're getting good at this! I bet that feels good." The self-concept problem will go away—eventually.

Focus on What's Right, Not What's Wrong

Many of us are programmed to react instead of think, thus we end up being overly critical with our teens. This contributes to their

self-doubt, by focusing on the negative. Ask yourself, "How can I come across in a more positive way?"

One way is to ask questions in place of giving orders. That doesn't mean interrogation. Ask a question and then say, "Is this what you mean?" or "Thanks for sharing that."

Long periods of silence between questions, and asking incomplete questions that give your teen the chance to fill in the blanks, can also be helpful.

Never Take Away What a Teen Can Do Well

Maybe your teen is not a great student, but is talented in sports. Wise parents encourage their teens to go after what they're best at with all they've got. This recharges their batteries and gives them strength to try things they're not as good at.

Treat Your Teen Like a Good Friend

It's amazing how we treat our family and loved ones sometimes. We often show our friends much more consideration and respect! When in doubt about how you're responding to your teen, ask, "How would I treat a good friend in this same situation?"

Adopt an Open "Mind-Set"

If we develop the mind-set that teens are tough to work with, we'll probably miss all the joys they offer—their creativity, sense of humor, and the fact that everyday is just a little bit different!

Raise the Odds in Favor of a Better Relationship with Your Teen

46

"I Know It's Your Room, But . . ."

HER EYES LOOK CAUTIOUSLY DOWN THE HALL. No footsteps. No voices. It seems safe. Her hand creeps slowly, tentatively, to the doorknob, despite the ominous warnings posted all around: "No Trespassing," "Keep Out," "Enter at Your Own Risk."

Sometimes a mom must risk personal safety in pursuit of a greater cause—even if that cause is nothing more than curiosity. She turns the knob and waits. Nothing. No booby-traps. No sirens. No mutant ninja warriors lunging to grab her throat. A welcome sigh of relief passes her lips.

Entering a child's room can be hazardous to your health. The condition of that room can be the cause of a great deal of parent/child friction. How much effort to expend on the "condition of the sty" really depends upon the age and responsibility level of the child.

Toddlers and preschoolers can be taught the joy of having a clean room by parental example. During the early years, parents can join the child in cleaning the room. If they do it, while talking out loud, it helps the child learn to feel good about doing the job. "Doesn't it feel good to get all of your stuffed animals in a row?" or, "I feel so much better now that I know you won't be eaten by those dust balls under your bed."

When we help our children clean their room, we send an unspoken message—there's a job, there's fun, and there's parents working with kids.

However, when our kids hit the third grade, it's time to step out of the picture. By offering choices and sharing the control, children can learn to be responsible for cleaning their rooms. It is important

that we avoid telling kids to clean up their rooms "right now". This sets up power struggles, passive resistance or defiance. Setting a time limit allows for choices, and gives parents much more control.

A conversation between parent and child might go like this:

DAD: "Would it be reasonable for you to have your room cleaned up by Saturday morning before we go to the amusement park? Everybody who has his or her room clean by then, gets to go."
SUE: "Aw, I don't want to clean my room."
DAD: "Well, that's okay. You don't have to. You can hire me or your sister or brother to do it. We'd love some extra cash. Or, you might want to hire yourself a baby-sitter for Saturday."
SUE: "But I don't have any money."
DAD: "When adults don't have any money, they sell something."
SUE: "Sell something?"
DAD: "Sure. But you don't have to decide right now what you're going to sell. You can tell me by Saturday. If you can decide by Saturday that means you get to choose what to sell. And if you can't decide, that means I choose. It's up to you."

Chances are, Sue will decide to clean her room. If not, she will surely learn an important lesson about how the world works. She can't lose.

❤

Avoid Power Struggles: Give Choices and Set Time Limits

47

"You're Grounded!"

IN THE REAL WORLD, the only time people are "grounded" is when they're locked up. Foster W. Cline, M.D., of the Cline/Fay Institute believes that grounding is usually ineffective for teens. It should be used after all other methods have failed—and only then, with great reluctance.

When parents give out heavy consequences like grounding, and then back off, they lose their teen's respect. Teenagers often refuse to obey them. We should never give orders we can't enforce.

There are better ways to handle a teen's behavior than grounding. Here are some ideas:

1. Express your concern to your teen— Letting teens know we are concerned with their actions is usually more effective in the long run than grounding. Let them know how their behavior is stressful to our relationship with them.

2. Make fewer, not more rules— There are three basic rules most teens need, but, outside of that, they should be given the chance to make their own decisions and live with their mistakes.

The three rules are:

1. Treat parents with the same respect you gave them in elementary school.
2. If you're of average intelligence, you get average grades.
3. Do your chores.

The best parents are those who are counselors. What they do best is listen and ask questions instead of giving orders.

3. Let natural consequences take over— Luckily, most consequences of behavior occur naturally. When teens get too many traffic violations, their licenses are taken away. If they drink and drive, their parents simply call the police.

There are other ways parents can let teens experience consequences. "Good guy" auto insurance, paid for by parents, is for teens who maintain good grades, receive no tickets, and pass driver's education. However, when a teen drives irresponsibly and gets poor grades, the parent says, "What a bummer, your insurance has gone up." The teen pays the increase in cost.

4. Take good care of yourself— This is a number one rule for parents. Adolescents learn far more from what they see us do than anything we tell them.

Instead of telling teens they can't drink and drive, a wise parent says, "You'll have to find some other car to drive and your own insurance. I can't take the chance my car will be in an accident involving drinking." Always follow through with your actions.

5. Think of solutions, not punishment— Wise parents often sit down and talk with their teens, rather than dish out punishments like grounding.

Today, many parents are coming up with solutions that include showing concern, reinforcing positive behavior, helping their teens reach their own conclusions, and letting natural consequences do the teaching.

❤

Grounding works best for those teens who need it least

48

Swearing and Bad Language

IT HITS US LIKE A TON OF BRICKS. That sweet and innocent child we're raising walks through the door one day spewing forth a string of expletives that knocks our socks off.

Sometimes kids use bad language because they want to be like their schoolmates. Sometimes they use it merely to test, or enjoy, our reaction.

In many cases, it is a mere rite of passage, a phase children go through. They hear older kids swearing and, wanting to be big like them, they develop a new vocabulary.

We could respond with demands, "You're not going to talk like that in this household! How many times have we told you to clean up that mouth?" Or, we could wash their mouths out with soap. Then they'd only resolve all the more to exert their independence, and that is seldom fun for us.

Solving this problem is a matter of taking small steps. The first step is to discuss where such language is acceptable, and second is to establish whether it is really necessary at all.

Step One
"You kind of like that word, don't you? You know, some kids like those words because when they use them their parents' mouths drop open. But the people who really know how to use those words are the kind of people who know where and when to use them. I'm curious about how much you know about that? What would you guess—when grandma's here for Sunday dinner? Would that be a good time to use those words? Or in your classroom? I'll be able to know how grown up you are by how well you can figure that out."

One place where they cannot use these words is around us. When the bad language comes out, we say, "Is this the right place for that language?" We repeat that question until we get results.

Step Two

The time to discuss this problem is when both the child and the parents are happy. One approach is to address the child's sense of worth: "You know, Leon, a lot of people who use that sort of language are people who don't feel that good about themselves."

We may want to take an intellectual tack: "People who use that sort of language are people with a very limited vocabulary, Leon. They don't know many words, so they pull out those boring old swear words and use them. Nobody will ever have to look them up in the dictionary. They're really easy words. You know, I can sort of understand people using them, Leon. So, if there's ever a day when you feel especially dim-witted and you come out with a couple of corkers, I'll try to understand that it's a time when you're feeling really crummy about your ability to use the English language."

Then we should drop the issue, the language our children use will, in the long run, be the language they want to use. White-hot anger on our part will only delay their realization that swearing is usually inappropriate.

❤

Discuss where swearing is acceptable and whether
it is really necessary

49

Isn't It Ever OK to Be Angry?

AS A GENERAL RULE, the decision on whether or not to use anger as we deal with our children, hinges on the issue of who owns the problem. Children's problems should always be met with empathy, sadness, or understanding. Empathy and sadness drive the pain of life's natural consequences deep into people's minds, so that real learning takes place.

If their mistakes only hurt *them*—if they trip and fall, or throw their fists and come home with a black eye, or skip half-a-dozen classes at school, then our anger only makes the problem worse. Youngsters concentrate on our anger to the point that they soon forget what they have done wrong. They become tied up with emotions such as guilt, or fear, and they have little time to think about ways to solve their problems.

When our kids do something that affects us directly—leaving their bikes in the driveway or failing to put our things away after using them—they will recognize that we're angry because their misbehavior has affected us. Anger, at this time, is a healthy emotion, as long as it is expressed in a healthy way. Many people use anger in an unhealthy way by accusing, threatening, and intimidating.

MOM: "Jerry! What is the matter with you? How many times have I told you to keep that bike out of the driveway? What do I have to do to make you understand how stupid that is? If I've told you once, I've told you a thousand times. Keep that bike out of the driveway, or I'm just going to drive right over it. I'm tired of this nonsense!
JERRY: "I'm sorry."
MOM: "Well don't do it again! I mean it this time!"

Compare this to the healthy way another mother describes her anger:

MOM: "Jerry, I'm mad! Every time you leave your bike in the driveway it makes a problem for me! I have to stop the car and get out! Today I had to get out in the rain! I don't want that to happen again!"

JERRY: "I'm sorry."

MOM: "That's what you said the last three times. It even makes me more angry to hear you say that you're sorry when it doesn't change how you act. If I see the bike out there again, I'll know that you want me to take it away until you are more responsible."

This mother's anger is effective because she is letting Jerry know how his actions affect *her* and how she is prepared to take care of herself if the behavior doesn't change. Jerry has not been personally attacked. He still had the chance to think about how he is going to solve the problem. He is not being told how bad he is, or how to correct the situation. This youngster is especially motivated, at this point, since mother is setting up a problem for him in the event he doesn't solve it.

The decision whether or not to use anger must be considered carefully. Generally speaking, it should be used only when our children's behavior directly affects us.

One note of caution, we should not use anger so often that it becomes an expected emotion. All of us, including children, love emotion. Once our child gets used to a particular emotion—be it shame, anger, guilt, or love—he/she finds ways to get us to express it often. This helps us understand the parent who says, "I don't know what's wrong with that kid. He just delights in making me mad!

Use anger only when your child's behavior directly affects you and you can do it without losing control

50

"That's an Option!"

"WELL, IF YOU GUYS DON'T LOVE ME ENOUGH to give me more allowance, I'll just have to start selling drugs!"

"I guess that's an option," said Mom.

"That's an option? What do you mean that's an option?"

Mom shrugged and said, "That's one way to solve your problem."

"You've got to be crazy! What are you on?" questioned Mark.

"Nothing," replied Mom. "Even though I love you more than anything in the world, the time has come when you have to decide for yourself how you are going to live your life."

"No way! You're on something. Otherwise you'd be giving me a lot of grief about this! Do you know that I could get caught for dealing? I could go to jail!"

"Don't worry. Maybe you'll make enough money dealing that you can hire some good lawyers to get you some light time. I'm sure you've thought it all out. Anyway, just think, if you get caught, the state will take care of you. You won't have to worry about allowance, room and board, or anything."

"Wait a minute! How am I supposed to go to college?"

Mom laid back on the couch and said, "Oh, you won't be in the slammer forever. With good behavior you'll get out and go to college later. You might even be better prepared because you'll have more life experiences."

"This is weird, man! Are you just going to sit there and let me ruin my life? Don't you even care about what happens to me? I can't listen to this! This is blowing my mind!"

And he stomped out of the room.

As far-fetched as this sounds, it is an actual conversation between a child and a parent who had learned to keep the monkey on the back of the child who owned the problem. She had learned that teens love to "hit" us, like Mark did in this situation.

The whole idea is to get the parent defending, advising, and demanding. Then the child goes into his/her judge role with statements such as, "That's not fair," or, "I can't do that." Before long the parent totally owns a problem the child actually needs to learn to solve.

Analyzing this situation, we see that the mother did not criticize Mark's thinking by saying, "That's stupid. Don't you dare do that!" She did not tell him what to do: "If you want to go to that concert badly enough, you'll get out and get yourself an honest job." And Mom did not use anger, guilt, intimidation, or orders such as, "As long as you live in my house you're not going to talk like that!"

This mother remembered that the response, "That's an option," will apply regardless of the stupidity of a teen's suggestion. A teen's inappropriate suggestion usually has parents doing all the thinking and ultimately taking over ownership of the problem.

The second skill Mom used was to think of all the advantages to Mark's solution of selling drugs. However, she stated them in rather negative, yet enthusiastic, terms. As you can tell from the dialog, it blew Mark's mind, and he switched into the role of telling her what was wrong with dealing drugs.

The third thing Mom knew was that Mark could learn from this type of dialog because she had a reasonably good relationship with him and things had gone well during his childhood.

❤

"That's an option," forces your teen to really think about what he/she has said

Chapter Six

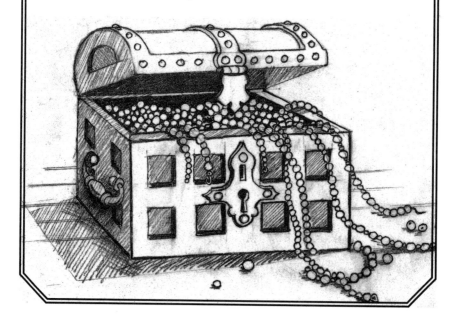

51

Sibling Rivalry

IT NEVER SEEMS TO FAIL. We can buy our children enough toys to start their own store, but when push comes to shove, one specific toy becomes the heart's desire of both of them. They tug and shove and shriek. They won't back down no matter what. It's a maddening phenomenon.

Normal parents, who have normal children, have children who fight. Sibling rivalry is a part of growing up. The thing to remember about dealing with our children's fights is to keep out of them. Expect them to handle it themselves. This may be the toughest parenting principle to follow, because children desperately want our intervention. In fact, our intervention makes it safe for them to fight. They know we'll step in before anyone gets hurt, so they have no qualms about putting up their dukes.

Our involvement in these spats should include only designating the location of the fight—somewhere away from us. As soon as the bickering starts to invade our ears, our youngsters are out of here. "Hey, guys, take it outside," is an effective way of dealing with squabbles.

Of course, we must step in if life and limb are in danger. If a big child continually terrorizes a small child—showing relentless anger toward him or her—then we need to stop it. Most of the time, however, we must remember that it takes two to tangle. Even the smallest and frailest child has ways to get to big brother or sister.

When the tongues have been stilled and fists unclenched, then and only then, do we counsel our children about fighting. Trying to reason with children who are emotionally upset is a waste of good air.

Helping our children solve their difficulties involves identifying their feelings. Were they feeling mad, sad, frustrated, left out, or something different? Why did they resort to angry words rather than

playing nice? First, they need to identify their feelings, and second, they need to identify different ways of handling them.

We can use modeling at this point: "If I hit my boss, Mr. Jackson, whenever I felt frustrated, I probably would not be as happy as if I handled my frustration another way." The point is, we must identify with the child's feelings, and then help the child work out a new course of action. However, it may be necessary to provide very stubborn children with a significant learning opportunity.

Adult and child psychiatrist, Foster W. Cline, M.D., tells of a counseling episode with a little boy named Kurt who was an expert at terrorizing other children. His modus operandi was simple, yet effective: He simply aimed for them on the playground and then mowed them down.

Two weeks after Kurt was placed in a good foster home, he and his foster mom came in for an appointment with Dr. Cline. The little lion had become a lamb. He gently held his foster mom's hand. Foster asked, "Kurt, how's the fighting going these days?"

"Oh, I'm not fighting much anymore," Kurt said.

"Well, why not?" asked Foster.

"Oh, because I hate doing all the chores."

Not understanding, Foster gave the boy a quizzical look. Kurt, seeing the perplexed look, explained, "Dr. Cline, when I fight, my mom says it drains energy from the family. But when I clean behind the refrigerator with a hand brush, that puts energy back into the family."

That explained it. In an untrained home, parents would have commanded Kurt to stop his behavior.

They would have said, "Kurt, don't you beat up on other children, or you'll regret it," and Kurt would have had his knees on the other child's arm before they finished the sentence. The foster mom had connected Kurt's behavior with a consequence. When Kurt's behavior deteriorated, she could look at him and say, "Kurt, honey, I feel an energy drain coming on," and Kurt would think, "Uh, oh, not that!" and there would be no fighting.

❤

Expect siblings to handle their own arguments themselves

52

Lying

Lying in childhood is a phase. However, if the phase is handled incorrectly by adults, the phase could develop into a life stance.

Many parents unconsciously make lying an issue by asking, "Is that the truth?" when there is really no solid reason to doubt the child. Sometimes when a child is dejected or down, parents may say, understandably, "What's wrong?" The child will say, not wanting to talk, "Oh nothing."

At this point, it is not wise for the parent to say, "Is that the truth?" or "Don't you fib to me," but to instead say, "Well if you want to talk, I'm here."

The most common mistake parents make, is to try and force their child to tell the truth when the parents already know the truth. This almost always ends in a control battle that neither parent nor child feels good about. Often the child continues to lie, getting deeper and deeper into negative feelings with the parent.

Here's how this parent avoids a control battle centered around stolen cookies by assuming the child knows the parent knows the truth of the situation:

PARENT: "Robert, come here. What did I tell you about these cookies?"
ROBERT: "Not to eat them; but I didn't."
PARENT: "What did I tell you?"
ROBERT: "Not to eat them."
PARENT: "Thank you! What did I say I was saving them for?"
ROBERT: "Paul's party."
PARENT: "Right. This hacks me off. You hit your room right now and think things over."

ROBERT: "But…"

PARENT: "Where do you need to go to think things over?"

ROBERT: "My room."

PARENT: "Thank you!"

If parents know the truth and try to get their child to admit it, it is a hidden way of saying, "I know you are going to continue to lie to me." When a child has lied, restitution needs to be made. The consequence is handled coolly and as nonemotionally as possible so that when our children do tell the truth about a difficult issue, we can say, "Wow, I bet that was hard to say! Thanks for the truth!"

The emotion we have as parents is best reserved for when the child says or does something right. Children can be "convicted" and consequenced on strong circumstantial evidence. Parents who find a candy wrapper in a child's room, and allow the child to protest that no candy has been eaten, are almost asking for the child to lie. A wise parent says, "I always take empty candy wrappers as evidence a person had eaten one. I think you need to give the whole thing some thought. If you still need to think about it over dinner time, no big deal."

Lastly, it is better to tell a child, "I don't believe you," than to say, "You're lying," It is easy for a child to argue he is telling the truth, but he can't argue with the fact that you don't believe him!

There are five basic rules for handling lying by children:

- Don't try to force your child to tell the truth when you already know it! Generally speaking, trying to force the child—ever—to tell the truth is a control battle the adult will lose.
- Give your child more positive emotion for being honest than negative emotion for lying.
- Consequence lying without anger.
- Children may be consequenced for circumstantial evidence.

❤

It's Better to Tell Children We Don't Believe Them
Than Tell Them They Are Lying

53

Reasonable Expectations for Adolescents

PARENTS OFTEN WONDER WHAT THEY SHOULD EXPECT from their adolescents. When parental expectations are too high, and limits are too tight, the adolescent becomes disrespectful and family communication and relationships can break down.

As adolescents grow older, parents must prepare their children for the *real* world; therefore, *real* expectations. Out in the real world, we are expected to get our job done, be respectful to others and, in general, be pleasant to be around. Thus, when children reach adolescence, wise parents have those same three rules, "I expect you to be respectful, responsible, and fun to be around."

In line with these expectations, parents may expect their adolescents to follow three simple rules:

1. Chores are to be done without being reminded.
2. The teen obtains average grades in school if they are of average intelligence.
3. When the teen is with the family, he/she is basically pleasant.

It is essential that real-world expectations flow back and forth between both parent and child. The child need not remind the parents to pay the utility bill and the telephone bill. Likewise, the parent should not be expected to remind the teen to do his or her chores. The teen is not expected to keep track of how the parent does their job at work. Likewise, it is fair for the parent to expect that the teen keep on top of the schoolwork and maintain average

grades. The teen does not keep track of the parent or choose the parent's friends. Likewise, if the teen is pleasant, responsible for his/her chores, and gets average grades in school, the parent should not be overly involved in the teen's life.

When children reach high school age, they basically use their home as a refueling pit, or base camp, for going off and exploring the world with friends. They often enjoy being with their friends more than they enjoy being with parents. Parents should not feel rejected. This is a stage of life. When parents rejoice in their teen's independence and refuse to get involved in rescuing when they make mistakes, most adolescents will respond by being thoughtful about their actions and appreciative of the independence offered.

Real-world expectations should be the same as
parent expectations for teens:
- Have chores done
- Maintain average grades
- Respect others and be pleasant to be around

54

When Parents Can't Agree on Raising Children

"BUT WHAT IF MY PARENTING STYLE IS DIFFERENT FROM MY SPOUSE'S? Isn't that going to be a problem for the children?"

This is a question often asked. Not to worry. Children adjust to the difference in adults almost instantly, when they know the parents will back each other. Having parents with two different parenting styles is not going to harm children. It becomes a problem only when one parent goes about trying to change the other one. This can become a serious problem because the children soon get wind of it and find themselves pitting the parents against each other.

It is rare for two parents to be in total agreement when it comes to raising children. This is all part of a grand design, whereby we usually marry a partner who has strengths in some areas in which we feel a little weak. This is usually great, until we have children and discover that the partner responds in a different way.

A typical scenario might go like this: Dad is a bit strict. Mom is a bit more lenient. Dad responds in a strict manner to two-year-old Erin, who immediately climbs up on Mom's lap for some sympathy. Mom says to herself, "Wow, Dad is too strict. I better balance it out by being more gentle and lenient." Dad sees this and says, "Look what a pushover Mom is. I'd better toughen up or this kid will get out of control." So, he becomes more strict.

In many families this begins a war of wills between two people who love each other. Each may be digging in his/her heels, afraid to give an inch for fear of admitting fault, or out of fear the child may be damaged.

Children sense this even when they don't hear the parents arguing about it. They start to view the world of big people as a place where you are supposed to square off against each other. The bad news is, children in these situations learn to square off against one parent and often manipulate as a way of driving a wedge between the parents. Worse yet, when they go to school, we find them manipulating teachers against teachers and parents against teachers.

Agree to Disagree

It would be ideal if both parents agreed on a parenting style; however, that is a rare situation. If you don't agree, remember that your children will develop a special and different relationship with each of you.

Talk with your partner, and agree that each of you will parent in your own way. Agree that you will never try to change each other, but, if the other comes to you asking for advice, you will relate what seems to work for you. Agree that if one parent starts to work with a child, the other will stay out of it. Agree that you will never criticize each other's parenting techniques in front of the children.

Be prepared for the children to complain about the treatment by the other parent. Many parents find it helpful to practice in advance, so a response is on the tip of the tongue. You might try, "Well, Dad has his own ways. I hope you learn to work it out with him." Or, "Mom must have her reason for doing that. Maybe it would be helpful for you to go back and talk to her about it."

♥

Individual parenting styles are OK as long as children know parents will back each other

55

Things Teens Don't Like to Hear

CONSCIOUSLY, AND GENERALLY UNCONSCIOUSLY, all of us like to hear, "I love you." That's probably the most important message in life. However, when raising children, the "I love you" message may be coupled with other messages that children may not, at first, appreciate.

The messages teens don't like to hear include variations of, "It looks like you have a problem." These messages drop the child's problem on his or her own shoulders. On the other hand, children like to hear parents make statements that show the parent is concerned, worried, or going to fix the problem for the child. Let's look at some of these messages.

Children like to hear parents say, "What am I going to do with you?" They don't like to hear parents say, "Gee, Henry, I hope you figure out what to do with yourself."

A child likes to hear a parent ask, "Am I going to have to . . . ?" The child, resistantly, answers, "Yeah, you're going to have to . . ." Children don't like to hear parents say, "I wonder if you need to . . ."

Once a parent says, "Am I going to have to . . . ?", they have given their youngster an all-time favorite response, for the child knows that he or she is in control of the situation. As teens like emotion, they love to hear parents say things like, "Am I ever *mad* at you." It's not nearly as much fun when a parent says, "Am I ever *sad* for you."

Then, there is the effective response to replace, "Gee, Henry, you have a problem." Telling a person that they have a problem can get old and it sometimes sounds uncaring. It is better to substitute, "Gee, Henry, good luck!" The "good luck" message, when given by a loving parent, means that the problem rests with the child.

We know children do not like to hear these messages because they respond with, "I hate it when you talk to me like that!" Or, "Have you been going to one of those parenting seminars again?"

Although these messages are, at first, upsetting to teens, they force teens to accept their own responsibilities. These teens will become happy and responsive individuals who take care of themselves.

❤

The statement: "It looks like you have a problem," forces teens to accept responsibility for their own actions.

56

When Death Hits Close to Home

WHEN TEENS LOSE SOMEONE CLOSE TO THEM—whether it is an immediate family member, a friend, or a close relative—the experience may be the first time death has hit so close to home.

In addition to the feelings of sorrow felt by people of all ages, a teen may be dealing with other intense emotions.

Some become consumed by guilt. If the death involved the suicide of a close friend or some type of accident, the teen may think, "Why didn't I do something to prevent this?" When teens lose a sibling, they may feel guilt over being the one spared from death. Some teens, particularly those predisposed to depression, may interpret the loss of a loved one as just one more sign that life isn't worth living. Others are stunned by the finality and reality of death.

Parents are encouraged to help teens cope with death in the following ways:

Accept Your Teen's Feelings

Grieving over the loss is natural. It is healthy for teens to be allowed to express their feelings of sadness and remorse, regardless of how the death occurred. Parents should not negate their teen's feelings with "I told you so," statements like, "If John hadn't been so reckless, he would probably be alive today."

Talk about Emotions

Parents should encourage teenagers to identify and talk about the emotions they are experiencing. Does the loss prove to them

that life is unfair? Are they holding themselves responsible? Are they angry because their friend caused his own death through foolish behavior?

When parents are experiencing the same loss, as in the case of the death of a family member, it is best if a teen talks with someone outside the family. A counselor, therapist or friend, who is not emotionally involved, can help a young person sort out and handle his or her feelings.

Death Is a Natural Process

A teen must learn to accept the reality of death as a part of the cycle of life. For the first time, some teens realize, "This could have actually happened to me!" For the first time, many recognize that life does not go on forever. In other cases, they recognize that death may be the consequence for the disregard of life.

After a teen has been given the time to deal with his or her immediate emotions of grief, parents may help the young person come to grips with reality through questions that encourage thinking. A parent asks his son, "Do you think Eric thought a lot about dying before his car accident?"

This question helps teens realize that their own behavior and thinking may also fit the profile of someone who is flirting with death.

Teens Cope Well When We Do

Children and teenagers generally handle life's difficulties only as well as their parents. If parents express their grief and sadness, while showing the ability to accept the loss, their children will generally follow their lead.

❤

Encourage your teen to identify and talk about the emotions he/she is experiencing

57

R-E-S-P-E-C-T

PARENTS ARE OFTEN CONCERNED BY THE LACK OF RESPECT shown them by their teenagers. This is a very important issue, for if parents allow their children to treat them with disrespect, it lowers the child's self-concept. Many parents, and even professionals, have this concept backwards. That is, professionals may tell parents that the child has a poor self-image and therefore the child treats them with disrespect. It is truly the other way around.

Sometimes parents have difficulty differentiating between a teen's assertiveness and disrespect or aggressiveness. Assertive behavior involves telling other people where we stand. Indeed, adolescents are very good at telling other people where they stand. That does not necessarily mean the adolescents are disrespectful. Aggressiveness, on the other hand, involves telling other people where to go. Adolescents should not be allowed to be aggressive with their parents. Disrespect also includes name calling, foul language, music played obnoxiously loud, and ignoring a parent who is trying honestly to relate.

It is essential for parents to understand their child's reasons for disrespect. Many adolescents are disrespectful because they are frustrated by unnecessary parental rules, regulations, and harangues. When teens feel their lives are unnecessarily controlled by adults, their only response is angry, impolite, and disrespectful comments.

In summary, parents must ask themselves, "Do I, or have I, treated my teen with disrespect? Am I confusing disrespect with protest or assertiveness? Am I consistently loving, and giving, my teen freedom to make his/her own mistakes?" If parents are able to

answer these questions to their own satisfaction, and their child continues to be disrespectful, then it is important to discuss the situation. A heart-to-heart talk must be carried out when the teen is in a good mood, and not immediately following an incident of disrespect. It does not help to try and solve a chronic problem when a chronic problem is occurring. The following conversation might take place:

PARENT: "Jack, how happy have you been at home recently?"
JACK: "I'm happy enough."
PARENT: "Well, I'm glad to hear that. I thought, considering the way you have been talking recently, you weren't too happy at home. I wonder if you might be happier living somewhere else?"
JACK: "Where would I go?"
PARENT: "Well, to tell the truth, I'm not sure. Do you know anyone who would find it fun to be around you right now?"
JACK: "Yeah, I've got plenty of friends."
PARENT: "I'm glad to hear that. That's one of our options, to see if some of those friends want to put you up for a while. Or, we can figure out how to talk and listen to each other. Let's each make a list of the ways we can make this situation better. Let's both give it some thought and share our lists after dinner."

Ultimately, if the parent is respectful to the teen, not infringing on his/her freedom and not confusing assertiveness with disrespect, the child will, in turn, be respectful. If the child continues to be disrespectful, it may be time to consider the tough love routine, with the emphasis on love. Out in the real world, no one puts up with chronic disrespect.

❤

Allowing a Child to Treat Adults with Disrespect
Lowers the Child's Self-Concept

58

Loss of a Loved One

PARENTS ARE OFTEN CONCERNED ABOUT THE PROPER WAY to handle death and dying with their children. What should the children be told about an afterlife? Are they too young to go to the funeral? Should they view the body?

Before the modern era, children naturally learned that death was an essential, and important, part of the life cycle. Children saw farm animals die all the time. Birth and death were seen as natural rhythms of life.

It is up to parents to combat the sanitized images of death so often seen on TV. Death naturally causes sorrow. Children should know this.

In coming to terms with Grandpa's and Grandma's death, with the death of a beloved pet, or with the death of parents, a growing individual should come to terms with his or her own death. However, in hiding both the sorrow and reality of death, parents can rob their children of the ability to cope and the ability to ask and deal with relevant questions.

Years ago, three children were killed by a lightning strike on a Colorado playground. There was talk about closing the school for a day of mourning. Cooler heads prevailed and this did not happen. Children must be taught that life goes on through the great cycles of both birth and death.

Generally speaking, children handle all of life's difficult issues as well as they are handled by the adults in their environment. This holds true for both divorce and death. Parents set the model for how children cope. If parents cope well, and expect that their children will cope, the children, heeding those expectations, cope well themselves.

No general rules can be given for the viewing of a body during a funeral. Many children, like many adults, would like to see Grandpa one last time. Other children, like some adults, would rather remember Grandpa the way he was, when he was vital and alive. It is an individual decision. If a child is six or older, these issues can be discussed and the children can decide for themselves. If children are under six, it generally does them no good at all to be around parents who are grief stricken and falling apart. It leads the child to feel insecure. If, on the other hand, parents are able to feel their sorrow, accept it, and cope with it while remaining loving and reassuring to the child, it may not be detrimental for the child to go to the funeral.

Finally, the manner in which every family handles life after death must be an individual matter. Generally speaking, it is helpful and thoughtful to give children hope. Young children feel reassured when a loving parent gives them a slightly Pollyannaish version of death: "When people are old, their body wears out and they think, 'My joints hurt, things don't work as well, I'll be glad when I get rid of this old body.'" It is correct to tell children, "When people are old, they often go to sleep and are ready to die."

As children get older, they will hear about heart attacks and people dying in pain; they will see it on television, and when they are ready, they will ask questions about it. Then, parents should handle the questions in an open and honest way, dealing with the situation in an age-appropriate manner.

❤

Children Handle the Difficult Issue of Death Only as Well as It Is Handled by the Adults in Their Environment

59

Teenage Depression

WHILE MOST YOUNG PEOPLE ARE ABLE TO WEATHER ROUGH TIMES, depression is not uncommon during the adolescent years, when teens are experiencing major life changes.

On the surface, a depressed teenager may appear angry. However, inside, he or she may harbor intense and overwhelming feelings of inadequacy, worthlessness, and hopelessness about both the present and the future.

Manic-depressive behavior is also an expression of teen depression. The onset of this condition can be perplexing and sudden. Among adolescents, it is most common in girls aged 14 and 15 who may exhibit out-of-character behavior, such as shoplifting, running up their parent's credit cards, or running off with boyfriends.

A parent may wonder if their teen's behavior is just a normal phase of growing up. When a teen's attitude gets progressively worse, showing no improvement over a three-month period, professional help is recommended. Parents should not view seeking professional counseling as an admission of their failure, they should see it as an opportunity to help their teen get through a painful time.

When a teen has been diagnosed with depression by a professional, the goal of parents should be to help their teen help themselves.

Follow Professional Advice

Teens who suffer from depression must accept the responsibility of helping themselves get better as soon as possible. They should be expected to follow the advice of professional counseling to the letter. That includes taking medication, if part of the treatment

plan, on schedule and without being reminded. Parents can help by assuring their teen that they will eventually improve.

Take Care of Yourself

While trying to help a son or daughter, parents must not let the teen's emotions rub off on them. Later, they must remain an island of stability in the face of the teen's mood swings. This means being understanding yet firm. A mother says to Lisa, "I really understand you're going through some painful times right now. But if you're having a bad morning, I'd prefer you work it out in your room."

Weigh the Options

In cases of severe depression, hospitalization may be recommended for your teen. A parent must judge whether this is a smart move. It helps if parents have developed a trusting relationship with the teen's psychologist or psychiatrist. Getting a second opinion is also a wise move, as is making sure that the person who recommends such treatment is *not* connected with the hospital.

When a teen's behavior causes major disruptions at home, a parent may decide it would be best if their son or daughter lived somewhere else for a time. When the parent/teen relationship is not strong, a teen may show improvement faster when living with relatives or family friends.

Parents also need to decide whether to be involved in their teen's therapy. When parents receive counseling at the same time, often the teen's condition improves faster.

Depression is curable. While living with a depressed teen can place unusual stress on a family, parents and teens can both be assured that the outlook for depression today is better than ever. Thanks to a better understanding of depression, along with new medications that offer dramatic results, the problem almost always improves with time.

❤

Parents must not let the teen's emotions rub off on them

60

"They're Calling Me Names"

PARENTS ARE UNDERSTANDABLY CONCERNED when their children are called names or teased for being different. Oftentimes, parents wonder, "Why does this happen? Why are children so mean to each other?"

Children call each other names, not to necessarily make others feel bad, but to make themselves feel good. As nationally known educational consultant Jim Fay explains, "children who are hurting inside want to make others hurt on the outside so that they can feel better about themselves."

Two Ways of Dealing with Name-Calling

When children are teased about being different, parents may handle it in two ways. First, some parents protect their child and talk to the children doing the teasing. This may be helpful in the long run, but it may covertly say to the child being teased, "You can't handle the situation, and you need help."

It's often better to strengthen the child, rather than try to lighten the load. Listening with empathy, as your child explains the situation, is a good way to start. Then teach the child "I messages" or ways to express how he/she feels, rather than telling them what the other person needs to do. A conversation with your child might go something like this:

PARENT: "What would happen if you told these children who pick on you to 'Cut it out!' Are they going to like you or get mad at you?"
CHILD: "Get mad at me."
PARENT: "Right. The trick is to tell them how you feel inside, not to tell them what's wrong with them. You might say, 'That makes me

feel pretty bad.' Does that say there is something wrong with them, or just tell them how you feel?"

CHILD: "How I feel."

PARENT: "Right. That's called an 'I'-message. You know how 'I' feel."

CHILD: "OK."

PARENT: "There's also a 'You'-message. 'You'-messages make people feel worse. If I say to you, 'Hey I don't like what you're doing,' is that a 'You'-message or an 'I'-message?"

CHILD: "'You'-message."

PARENT: "Right. Tell them how you feel inside. Be nice about it, but tell them exactly how you feel. So, you are going to send what messages?"

CHILD: "'I'-messages."

PARENT: "And you're not going to send...?"

CHILD: "'You'-messages."

Nothing we say to our children can take away the hurt of their being teased. However, we can help them cope with, and handle, the hurt appropriately. We let them know that there will be many other hurts in their lives, and we are certain that they will be able to cope with those too.

❤

When your children are being picked on:
Listen with empathy—Teach the use of "I"-messages.

Chapter
Seven

61

Getting Kids to Do As Asked

"THIS KID IS DRIVING ME CRAZY! You'd think she could do the few little things I ask her to do without having to be reminded over and over! I don't know what is the matter with her!" It's not uncommon to hear frustrated parents talking like this. The good news is, it doesn't have to be this way.

Parents who have the most difficulty getting their children to do things generally fall into three categories:

1. Parents who do not follow through with a consequence when their child fails to perform— The most effective parents don't demand that their children do something, until they have first thought of what they will do if the child doesn't accomplish the task. Ineffective parents often give an order, wait to see if it will be carried out, and then, start hoping that they can think of a consequence. Too late! Times of frustration, disappointment, or anger are terrible times to come up with effective consequences that need to be delivered in nonangry ways.

2. Parents who make idle threats and/or reminders— Children know how to handle this kind of parent. Some children don't comply. Some feel obliged to resist doing as told, just to see if the parent is actually going to do anything about it. Some comply, but complete the job only halfway. Regardless of the way the child handles it, the parent ends up frustrated and the child's feelings of responsibility and competence are damaged.

3. Parents who say, "Do it now!"— Children have a subconscious preference for this approach. They just seem to instinctively

know that a parent can never win this one. Just knowing that a parent can never make you "do it right now!" gives a child a sense of power. Children who don't feel a healthy level of personal control, learn that they can overpower adults just by "dragging their feet," and saying through their actions, "You can't control me."

The Solution Is a Reasonable Deadline

STEP 1: Never say, "Do it now." It is always more effective to say, "I'd appreciate you picking up your room by 5:30 p.m. Thank you." Remember to add the "thank you" in advance. It shows that you don't expect less than pleasant compliance.

STEP 2: Don't remind! Hope that the job does not get done. Your youngster can then have an opportunity to see that something actually happens when he/she doesn't cooperate. Keep the possible consequence a secret, so that it can come when least expected, just like a lightning bolt out of the sky.

STEP 3: At precisely 5:31 p.m., pick up the room and put the clothes and toys where they can't be found.

STEP 4: When the child asks about his/her things, say, "Oh, the clothes and toys? They didn't get picked up on time so they're gone. Every time you do something helpful around here, without being told, you can earn one of them back. It will be fun to see what you decide."

❤

Set a Reasonable Deadline and Don't Remind

62

Four Steps to Responsibility

AS A GRADE SCHOOL PRINCIPAL, educational consultant Jim Fay, often woke in the mornings scared for those children who never got into trouble. Now, that may sound like an odd fear, but Jim knew from experience that well-behaved youngsters would eventually leave school a lot less prepared for the real world than those children who had learned lessons through occasional misbehavior.

Preparing students for the "real world" is one of the greatest gifts we can give our children. It means teaching them responsibility and decision making at a young age.

Building Responsible Children

Parents can help children "practice" for the real world by adopting Four Steps to Responsibility:

STEP 1: Give your child a responsibility

STEP 2: Hope your child makes a mistake— If we don't allow our children to make mistakes, and then live with the consequences, we are really "stealing" valuable learning experiences from them. Today's mistakes—forgetting to finish their homework or leaving their lunch at home—are bargains compared to what mistakes may cost as they grow older.

STEP 3: Allow empathy and consequences to do the teaching— Learning never takes place from parental anger. Instead, use empathy when you talk with your children, to allow them to look closely at their decisions.

STEP 4: Give the same responsibility again— This is the most important step. It sends a powerful message to the child that he or she is smart enough to learn from the previous mistake.

Essential Decision-Making Skills

Problem-solving and decision-making skills are the building blocks of responsibility. Most children don't get much practice at it. They also don't have the advantage of actually seeing the process adults use to make decisions.

We can help children learn how to solve their own problems by following these steps:

1. Show understanding.
"I bet that really hurts."

2. Ask questions.
"How do you think you're going to work that out?"

3. Get permission to share ideas.
"Would you like to hear what some other children have tried before?"

4. Help the child explore possible consequences.
After every suggestion ask . . . "and how do you think that might work?"

5. Let your child "solve" or "not solve" the problem.
Wish the child "good luck" with his or her decision.

63

Gangs and Cults

THE DRAMATIC INCREASE IN THE NUMBER OF GANGS AND CULTS is a sad reminder of how things have changed in America. Hardly a day goes by in many urban areas without disturbing news of violent events that too often include death.

Unfortunately, gangs and cults are expected to grow in popularity as the role of the family continues to weaken. Where the family once served as a young person's gang, the gang has now become the family for some of our children.

Young people turn to gangs and cults when their needs aren't being met in their own families. A gang or cult is a substitute, with a powerful attraction, offering fulfillment of a child's need for trust, sharing, control, affection, excitement, and inclusion.

Strengthen the Family Unit

How do we stop children from joining gangs and cults? The best way is to provide a strong and supportive family that recognizes and meets a youngster's needs.

A sense of control is experienced by children who are given enough room to grow. Wise parents teach their children, beginning at an early age, to make their own decisions and then live with the consequences of those decisions.

Parents who are threatened by a child's actions, often respond by giving that child fewer choices. This almost always creates an even stronger need for young people to assert themselves. Consequently, the youngster spends more time defending him/herself than thinking about the consequences of the choices.

Parents who encourage youngsters to develop their talents and interests, also build the child's self-confidence. Self-confident children are rarely interested in gangs or cults. A child with a weak self-image is much more likely to be attracted to a gang or cult in order to achieve the sense of self-fulfillment he or she lacks.

The same basic attractions of a gang or cult can be found in many nondestructive ways, including sports, clubs, and even school. Wise parents help their youngsters build a strong self-image through heavy involvement in activities such as skating, track, drama, football, art or music, to name a few. Even in inner cities, where opportunities are limited, a child's "gang" may be found on the basketball court.

There is little parents can do to control a young person's behavior outside the home. When a child threatens to join a gang or cult, it's best to express your concern while making sure the child understands you are unwilling and unable to rescue him/her from dangerous situations.

Youngsters often discount their parents' wishes, but will listen to other adults. The words of someone outside the home, such as a school counselor, are usually taken far more seriously and may help a young person understand the dangers involved in gangs and cults.

There is no magical way to guarantee that a child will stay clear of a gang or cult. Parents can reduce the possibility of this activity by ensuring their own family can "compete" with the attractions gangs and cults offer.

❤

Gangs and Cults Serve as a Substitute Family

64

Angry Kids

"WHY DOES MY CHILD ALWAYS HAVE AN ATTITUDE? She's often disruptive, disrespectful, or picking on other children. She's always the one with a chip on her shoulder." This frustrated parent expresses the feelings of many—Why is my child angry and how do I deal with it?

A child who acts out may be expressing other emotions through anger. A youngster may be experiencing a loss, a divorce, or a move. A child may be trying to let the world know that his/her life is not what it ought to be. Regardless of the reason, it looks the same. How can we deal with this angry attitude without being a psychologist?

Listening for understanding is impossible when a child is "drunk" on anger. Never reason with an angry child. Instead, say, "It sounds like you're really mad. I want to listen and understand. I will listen when you're voice is as calm as mine. Come back then." If you can't make the child leave, you leave.

Be prepared to repeat your calm statement, if the child is determined to yell out the anger without leaving. "Don't worry about it now. We'll talk when you're calm." You may need to say this several times. Be prepared to play "broken record" with, "What did I say?" Use these phrases instead of reasoning. Reasoning will only fuel the anger.

"Thanks for Sharing That"

Once the child is able to discuss the anger, listen without reasoning. Try to avoid telling the child why he/she should not be angry. Avoid telling them that things will be okay and how to make it better. Your job is to prove that you understand—"It sounds like

you get mad when I tell you it's time to do your chores. Thanks for sharing that with me. I'll give it some thought. If you think of a better way for me to ask you, let me know."

Parents Can Make It Worse

Parents who do not treat their children with respect send a message that says, "You're not worthy." These parents often communicate with a lot of yelling. This encourages the child to yell and scream back, while the parents retaliate by getting more mad. It's a vicious cycle that breeds chronic anger in the child.

In place of anger, parents should work on listening to their children in a nonthreatening, honest, and open manner. Most children will talk openly only after they truly believe their parents are interested in what they have to say and recognize their feelings.

When Anger Continues

If, despite your best attempts to understand your child's anger, there is no change in behavior after three months, parents should seek professional counseling for their child. In some instances, chronic anger is best helped by a professional.

Never reason with an angry child. Use empathy and understanding instead.

"It sounds like you're really mad. I want to listen and understand. And I will listen when your voice is as calm as mine. Come back then."

❤

A Parent's Job Is to Understand, Not to Fix Things

65

Raising Daredevil Kids

NO DOUBT THE WORLD IS A DANGEROUS PLACE. Every day the head-lines tell us of more violence. In some larger cities, cars are even being stolen while people are *in* them.

So, it is understandable that most parents feel less than secure about the well-being of their children. Because there are more prob-lems, parents may become more watchful, careful, and protective. In fact, I have seen parents who are so vigilant in watching their chil-dren, that simply "being vigilant" could be their full-time job!

It is understandable that daredevil children raise vigilant parents. However, there is an easier way. *Teach the child to be vigilant!*

How do we do that? First, consider the three types of children:

1. Children who would never be "daredevilish" and never take risks.
2. Death-defying little daredevils, who are at high risk. Death does not like to be defied very long!
3. Daredevils who take thoughtful risks, and whose chances of being hurt are slight.

This last group of children might be likened to trapeze artists, who, when performing amazing stunts on the flying trapeze, use a safety net. In other words, what they do looks pretty daring, but is really pretty safe.

Children must be taught, when they are two or three years old, to be thoughtful daredevils, not death-defying daredevils. This is the stage of toddlerhood exploration. This is when parents start raising the three types of children listed above, and then who, in turn, will have their own buttons pushed by the child.

The first child— a child who timidly partakes of life and never takes risks, is raised by a parent who is constantly worried, giving messages such as:

"Be careful, you'll get hurt. Oh, John, you scared the wits out of me! Please don't do that!"

The second child— the child who may be at risk of death, usually is raised by frightened parents who show their worry with anger. When the child takes small risks in toddlerhood, the mother or father may angrily state:

"Stop that right now or you'll get a swat! You make me so mad when you take those chances!"

The third type of child— a little daredevil who takes thoughtful risks, is raised by a parent who states:

"If you do that, you might get hurt." (The parent then does not rescue.)

"John, honey, the way you are behaving, this could be good-bye. If you kill yourself, I would miss you!"

In essence, the message the first parent gives the child is, "The world is a scary place, and I'm frightened for you."

The second parent, raising a rebellious and foolish child, says, "The world is a dangerous place, and I'm mad at you!" All children, on an unconscious basis, like to make their parents angry. They really can't help themselves!

Finally, the third parent says, "The world may be a dangerous place, so I hope you watch out."

A word of caution as we watch our daredevil kids at play:

Generally, we can sit back and make reasoned, thoughtful comments, unless they are doing something that is likely to cause serious injury or death, then immediate action is called for.

This is an issue that has to be carefully weighed, for the more severe the consequences, the more memorable the learning experience. We don't want the child to remember it from heaven!

❤

Teach the child to be vigilant!

66

Life after High School

MOST PARENTS BEGIN THINKING ABOUT LIFE AFTER HIGH SCHOOL before their children can even walk. "Doesn't Johnny look just like a Stanford graduate," a parent exclaims about her toddler. As much as parents want their children to succeed, it often backfires when they try to choose their child's destiny.

Exploring Options

Wise parents explore future alternatives with their teen. It's best to make sure teens are thinking about the future while still in high school.

Your teen may feel a lot of pressure surrounding this issue. Those who want to attend college, may worry about grades, test scores, and finances. They, along with those who don't know what they want, are in need of their parent's support. A mother demonstrates her support with these words: "Heidi, I know it'll be two years before you graduate, but if you'd like some help thinking about what to do after high school, I'd love to talk with you. You have so many talents and interests that will really help you in life."

Another parent says to Jamie, "Since you're so interested in business, have you thought about talking to a career counselor to learn about the skills you'll need for such a career?"

Teens Who Live at Home

Young people have several options after high school. They may attend a university, junior college, or trade school, or choose to find a job. Others may need to work while attending college to finance their education.

A "free ride" is not an option. Wise parents have taught their teens that nothing in life is free. Then, it comes as no surprise, when they are expected to contribute to the household, should they continue living at home after graduation and are not attending school.

There's nothing wrong with allowing teens to live at home, as long as they pay rent and the arrangement is beneficial to the parents. A parent might say, "I will provide you with the best deal on rent you can get anywhere. In return, I expect you to be thoughtful, respectful and positive to be around."

Parents who do not require rent payments, encourage a dependent relationship in which teens do not take charge of their lives.

Let Your Teen Grow Up

Parents should avoid the temptation to solve the dilemma of a young person's future. They may be supportive by providing their thoughts and financial assistance for education, if they can afford it. Parents, however, are not responsible for arranging jobs for their teens or for choosing their majors. While our children may not become exactly what we want them to be, we must recognize that they must only live up to their own expectations.

❤

Wise Parents Explore Future Alternatives with Their Teen

67

Helicopters, Drill Sergeants, and Consultants

HELICOPTERS, DRILL SERGEANTS, AND CONSULTANTS may sound like unlikely titles for parents, but a closer look reveals the kinds of messages these different parents send to their children.

Helicopters

Helicopter parents make a lot of noise, a lot of wind, and a lot of racket. They hover over and rescue their children whenever trouble arises. Often viewed as model parents, they sincerely believe they are preparing their children for the real world.

However, helicopter parents are actually "stealing" learning experiences from their children in the name of love. The message sent to the child is, "You are fragile and can't make it without me."

Drill Sergeants

Drill sergeant parents also make a lot of noise, wind, and racket. Their motto is: "When I say jump, you jump!" The children of drill sergeants, like those of helicopters, have never had the chance to make their own decisions and are dependent upon their parents. The message sent by drill sergeants is, "You can't think for yourself, so I'll do it for you."

Consultants

Consultant parents are always willing to give advice. Instead of rescuing or controlling, they allow their children to make decisions

and experience life's natural consequences, while providing guidance. Consultants are always willing to help children explore solutions to problems. They're always willing to describe how they would solve a problem themselves. Then they "blow out" and allow their children to make their own decision. Instead of dependency, the consultant sends messages that create self-worth and strength in their children.

The following example indicates the difference in these three styles:

When a child complains about being picked on at school, the helicopter says, "Don't worry, I'll tell the teacher to straighten that kid out for you." The drill sergeant commands, "You smack that kid the next time and he'll stop!" The consultant replies, "That's really sad. Would you like to hear what some other kids have done to solve that?"

❤

GUIDANCE SERVICES
Think of a consultant parent as someone who provides guidance services for their children. The following will help you become a consultant parent:
- Take care of yourself
- Provide alternatives
- Allow natural consequences to take place

68

"The Quick-Fix Attitude"

CHILDREN ARE BOMBARDED, at an early age, by television ads and sit-coms that imply there are magic solutions to all of life's problems. Unfortunately, this is not the case. However, this "quick-fix" attitude has prompted children to believe there's always an easier way. Such an attitude can influence the way we see our "self-movies."

Self-Movies

Our subconscious mind functions much like a video player. When a friend calls and says, "Let's go skiing," a little movie flashes through our head. This is called a self-movie. We either see a positive self-movie—we picture ourselves being successful and having a good time. Or we see a negative self-movie—we picture ourselves making constant mistakes and falling on the ski slopes. The movie we see, actually determines whether or not we go skiing.

The same thing happens when children are asked to do a school assignment. A movie plays about their possible success or failure. Children who see themselves doing well and feeling good about the assignment, are willing to try. Those who see a negative self-movie, appear as if they don't care about success. This is their protective shield, but it looks like an attitude problem.

Children who frequently see negative self-movies are easily discouraged. They begin to see more negative self-movies as opposed to positive self-movies showing success and good feelings. These children become less willing to risk. They are often the ones who live lives in which they aren't required to earn things they want, and don't have to make frequent struggles to accomplish chores.

They watch lots of examples of magic solutions on television. These are the kids who are victims of the "Quick-Fix Attitude."

Changing the Movie

This self-movie can gradually change from negative to positive. Here's how:

Limit criticism— Children who live with critical parents, soon take over the criticism for themselves. Many adults, in therapy, talk about how their parents were always correcting them when they were children. Most say, at one point in their lives, they started to hear their own voice doing the same thing, "I never do anything right." "I'm so slow." "I know I can't do it." "I'm so dumb." People like this are constantly seeing negative self-movies and are afraid to try anything new.

Make it safe to take a risk— Children who feel safer about taking risks, have overheard their parents talking with each other saying, "I'm so glad I tried that. I felt foolish at first, but I had a great time. I'm so glad I don't have to be perfect the first time to have a good time." This parent is a good model, who knows their children learn from what they see, not what they are told.

Support new activities— Do all you can, without being pushy, to encourage children to experiment with new activities. Many people never discover their hidden talents because they are afraid to try.

It's also important that children hear enthusiastic statements from their parents when they put out the effort to try something new, even in the face of a negative self-movie. Children need to hear, "I bet you feel proud that you tried it anyway!"

❤

Self-Movies Can Gradually Change from Negative to Positive

69

Stealing

"OH NO, DOES THIS STEALING INCIDENT MEAN MY CHILD is headed for a life of crime?" Few behaviors are more upsetting to parents than stealing. Even occasional stealing by a child causes parents considerable concern.

Like lying, stealing is almost always a childhood phase. Children aren't necessarily practicing for a career in crime! Most outgrow the behavior, if their parents handle the situation calmly, by praising a child for returning stolen objects instead of becoming enraged at the actual act of stealing.

Let Consequences Teach

Most children will change only when they realize the satisfaction they get from stealing isn't worth the consequences they must pay for their behavior. Consequences, provided with empathy and sadness in place of anger, go a long way in helping children think about their actions.

When Travis is caught stealing art supplies at school, Dad provides plenty of empathy, while making sure Travis feels the consequences.

DAD: "I'm sorry to hear you're in trouble at school. I'll bet that makes you feel real bad."

TRAVIS: "Yeah, my teacher says I can't use the art room for a whole month!"

DAD: "I'm sorry for you son, and even though I love you, your teacher is doing the right thing. It's not fair to others when you take

things from the classroom. Maybe you'll be able to finish your projects next month. I think that's up to you."

Chronic Stealing

When stealing becomes chronic behavior, parents must try to understand the reasons behind this undesirable activity.

Children who steal often feel empty and unloved. Unlike adults, who have several positive or negative ways to fill emotional voids, children have few avenues to remedy the pain and emptiness they feel. Stealing by a child can be translated into the words, "I'm not getting my fair share." It provides temporary relief from the empty feeling; therefore, the behavior may become a habit.

Chronic stealing is a symptom of underlying problems. The solution usually is found in helping the child feel more loved, accepted, and recognized.

Spend Extra Time with Your Child

Plan a special time each week to give your child your undivided attention. Whether you take a walk, play one of your child's favorite games, or just nuzzle and watch TV together, you will be helping to fill the void your child might be feeling.

Teachers can be enlisted to help by increasing the amount of daily eye contact and recognition provided to your child. You can also request that the teacher avoid unnecessary humiliation of your child, by keeping the consequences for stealing a private matter between the teacher and student.

When Stealing Continues

If, after three or four months, you see no change in your child's behavior, professional help may be needed to help identify the underlying reasons for the stealing.

❤

Most children will change only when they realize the satisfaction they get from stealing isn't worth the consequences

70

Parent/Teacher Conferences

PARENT/TEACHER CONFERENCES CAN BE AN EMOTIONAL TIME for both parties. It's not unusual for either parents or teachers to forget they are really on the same team—the child's team!

When both parties put forth their best communication and listening skills, these emotional battles can be replaced by the opportunity to share ideas that are in the student's best interest.

Conferences That Are Guaranteed to Fail

When teachers and parents come to a meeting with a set notion of the child's problem and how to deal with it, the result is often a contest of words. Both parent and teacher waste a lot of time trying to persuade the other to understand and adopt their point of view.

The following are proven techniques that can end any progress during a conference:

Nonnegotiable demands— A parent who demands, "I want Rachel transferred to a different reading group by Monday!" has effectively put an end to communication.

Threats— A teacher who threatens, "If Danny disrupts my class one more time, I'll send him to the principal's office every day for the rest of the month!" has not learned the art of either negotiation or communication.

Accusations— The statement, "If you would give Johnny more personal attention at home, his reading skills would be up to speed," is guaranteed to put a parent on the defensive.

Words That Work Wonders

Parents and teachers alike must remember the reason for meeting is to share ideas that will help the child overcome his or her school problems. People who get the best results during these conferences remember the magic words of good communication.

Describe the problem— When we use the word "describe," we open lines of communication by eliminating any judgmental statements. A wise parent says, "I'd like to describe how I see the problems Susie has been having in your class." A smart teacher says, "I'd like to describe how Lee acts around his classmates during recess."

Ask for the other person's thoughts— "I'd like to get your thoughts on that," are also magic words. They show we are more interested in learning all we can about the child's problem rather than trying to persuade the other party to see our side. The words also imply that we respect the other person's opinions.

Listen to the other person— Effective communication takes place only when people are convinced the other person is truly listening to them. Neither parent nor teacher should interrupt the other. Both need to be confident that their perceptions are being heard.

Develop several solutions— Coming up with more than one alternative to a problem—together—eliminates the temptation of trying to convince the other person to see the problem your way. It shows sincerity and openness about helping the child.

Remember! Parents and Teachers Are on the Same Team—
the Child's Team!

Chapter Eight

71

How to Give Your Kids an Unfair Advantage—Part I

SUSIE CAME FROM ASIA AS AN ADOPTED CHILD. She joined a family with solid values, relating to achievement and personal responsibility. In a few short years, she had moved to the head of her class.

Her classmates at school periodically asked her about why she got high grades. They thought it was because Asians usually excel at academics. Her answer was that she always did her homework before she went out to play.

Susie became the valedictorian and gave the address at the graduation ceremony. This caught the attention of many parents of the other children. "Why is this?" they asked.

One couple actually called Susie's parents to try to discover the answer. Susie's father mentioned that they shared the values of hard work, struggle, and personal responsibility. He said Susie was expected to be responsible, and when she was not, natural consequences were applied. He also mentioned that their expectations were that Susie would do her chores, be respectful of her parents, and apply herself to her schoolwork.

"Susie knows where we stand," said Dad. "She knows that in America she has the right to life, liberty, and the pursuit of happiness; not the right to life, liberty, and someone else to provide happiness for her. Susie is busy pursuing her own happiness through achievement and personal responsibility."

"Wait a minute!" replied the other parents. "Doesn't that give her an unfair advantage over the other children? Come on, Mr.

Tyler. This is America. Whatever became of equal opportunity?"

"I guess if you look at it that way, there may never be equal opportunity. As long as some people work harder than others and place a high value upon achievement through struggle, they will always have an advantage over the others. I guess that's the America I know."

America's founding fathers dedicated our nation to life, liberty, and the pursuit of happiness. Americans knew they had a chance for success through struggle, and as a result, struggle made America great. Over the years, we have gradually moved toward an attitude of protecting our children from struggle. Many parents have said, "I don't want my children to struggle like I did. I want them to have a better life and all the things I never had."

The results of this are being seen in our public schools, as fewer and fewer children appear to be willing to accept struggle as a necessary part of learning. Teachers are working harder and harder to find new ways to motivate students, who often believe the teachers are being mean by asking them to struggle.

The schools are being criticized because children are not achieving as well as in the past. However, changing the schools will not solve this problem. America will be plagued with underachieving students until our entire society changes its message about the value of struggle. That's the bad news.

The good news is that your child can stand out and have a real advantage over others—by learning to struggle and to be responsible early in life. When teachers challenge kids who have struggled, those kids think, "No big deal. I'm not afraid to struggle. In the end, I'll be successful."

In Part II, we'll explore some very specific techniques, which, when put into practice, can give your child the advantage. These tried and true approaches will help you stay out of power struggles with your children and, at the same time, convince them that their success depends upon the quality of the decisions they make.

Expect your child to be responsible, and when they're not,
apply natural and logical consequences

72

How to Give Your Kids an Unfair Advantage–Part II

In Part I we explored the advantage children gain by being given the opportunity to struggle. In this article we'll explore specific techniques that parents can use to give their children a head start in life.

Give chores— Regardless of what your children say about chores being unfair or that none of their friends have to do chores, children need to contribute to the welfare of the family.

To get your children performing their chores, begin by spending a couple of weeks listing all the jobs that have to be done for the family to survive. This list should include all the jobs parents usually do, as well as, the things children need their parents to do for them. Have your kids select the jobs they think they would most like to do. In the event they don't like any of the jobs, have them choose the ones they hate the least.

A proven technique for getting children to do their chores is to say, "There is no hurry each day to do the jobs. Just be sure they are done before the end of the day." Do not remind them about the chores. If the jobs are not done by the end of the day, say nothing and let the kids go to bed. Let them sleep for 30 to 45 minutes and then wake them up, reminding them that the end of the day is near and they are to get up and finish their work. Don't take "no" for an answer.

Provide matching funds— Kids are bombarded with media advertisements about their need for material things. It is tempting to give them all you can as a show of love. It may also be tempting

to say, "You don't need those things." Both of these responses rob the child of a chance to struggle.

Times when children ask you to buy something are opportunities to provide success through struggle. This is the time for the parent to implement "matching funds." Tommy announces, "I really need those basketball shoes. All the other kids have them and they're only $125."

The wise parent responds, "You ought to have them. I can't wait to see how you look in them. I'll contribute $35. As soon as you earn the rest, you'll have those shoes."

CHILD: "But it's not fair. The other kids' parents buy them."
PARENT: "I know. It's rough living the way we do. Let me know when you're ready for the $35."

Tommy will wear those new shoes with greater pride once he has struggled to earn them.

Your value system should dictate the amount you provide each time. Sometimes you contribute 75%, sometimes 10%, and sometimes you might even contribute 90%. There is no firm rule. Remember that a gift once in a while doesn't hurt a thing.

Don't pay for good grades or punish for bad grades— As long as children have others who will worry about their problems, they don't worry about them. It's as if they say, "My parents have that worry well in hand. No sense in both of us worrying about it." Parents who offer to pay for good grades, or punish for bad ones, are taking over too much of the worry about grades. This also raises the odds the child will see achievement as something that is being coerced rather than offered.

Once a youngster sees grades as part of a power struggle, the issue is no longer the value of a good education, but who is going to win. A child in a power struggle can see only one choice: winning the power struggle. However, as long as a child has two choices, to succeed or not to succeed, there is still a good chance of success.

❤

Children, who earn what they get gradually, learn self-respect, resourcefulness, the value of money, and most importantly, that problems are solved through struggle.

73

"You Wouldn't Care if I Never Came Home!"

Teens who threaten to run away should be taken seriously. Even if, deep down, they have no intention of actually carrying out the threat, the words are almost always a sign of problems in the parent/teen relationship.

Teens threaten to run away for a variety of reasons. When they don't get their way, some try to manipulate their parents. Others use the statement, "You wouldn't care if I never came home," to express that they are feeling unloved. Some teens run away to build better lives, by escaping an unhappy family situation.

Examine the Parent/Teen Relationship

When a teen threatens to leave, parents should determine whether their own actions are contributing to the adolescent's discontent. It's best to enlist someone outside the family, such as a counselor, who can evaluate the situation objectively. Are the parents too critical? Do they accept their teen's need for independence? Do the parents recognize that their teen needs fewer, not more, rules? Do they take the time to listen to, and talk with, their son or daughter?

When parents and teens make the commitment to improve their relationship through better communication, the issue of running away may disappear.

If You Can't Control, Plant a Seed of Thought

If the parent/teen relationship is basically good, a teen's threats are probably manipulative in nature.

Although parents can't prevent their youngsters from running away, the chances of this behavior taking place are reduced when teens are required to think about their actions.

A parent says to her teen, "If you want to run away, that's your choice, even though I hope you'll choose to stay home and work things out. But, if you do run away, I hope you'll stay away long enough to find out if that's what you really want."

Another parent says, "If you choose to run away, please feel free to return only when you are really sincere about working out problems here at home."

Most teens who run away have every intention of returning. Most hope their parents are spending all their time worrying about them. Parents can let their teens know that if they run away, they must be prepared to face, and pay for, the consequences, including lawyer fees and possible youth detention.

Determine the Expectations

When a teen runs away and then returns, the parents and teen must try to work things out through a list of written expectations. Teens then become aware of their long list of needs, including a home, food, money, and use of the family car.

When parents and teens compare the two lists of expectations, the teen may realize their parents aren't as unreasonable as they thought.

❤

Wise parents have only three basic expectations
of their sons and daughters:
• Treating their parents with respect
• Doing their chores without being reminded
• Getting average grades in school, if they are of average intelligence

74

Parent/Student Stresses

WE LIVE IN ENORMOUSLY COMPLEX TIMES. Few of us are immune to the stresses and pressures that are a part of the landscape of our fast-paced society.

A recent study showed that Americans, on the average, have 30% less free time than they enjoyed just a decade ago. Stress is no stranger to families who find themselves bound by limits on both their time and energy.

When our children become teenagers, family stress may increase even more. Parents find themselves with more to worry about—including issues like drugs, teen pregnancy, grades, and even guns in the school. It is a time, when some begin to doubt their ability to parent.

Teens today are also under a lot of pressure. They are in the midst of major social, emotional, and physical changes that are a part of growing up. They are also faced with important decisions to make about almost every aspect of their lives.

Although we can't eliminate all pressures that are a part of our society, we can do our best to control the stress levels within our own families. This becomes possible, when we realize that communication problems between parents and teens can create additional stress.

The following guidelines are designed to help parents manage and reduce stress within the family:

Respect each other's needs— The way our own parents raised us may no longer apply to today's generation of young people. Today's teenagers are encouraged to both establish their indepen-

dence and stand up for their rights as individuals. Some parents, threatened by this behavior, clamp down harder, creating an even stronger need for teens to assert themselves.

Respect is a two-way street. Teens must also learn to respect their parent's needs. However, if the parent is respectful of the teen, the child can see what respect looks like.

Encourage an open relationship— Both teens and parents have limited time. However, it's a good idea to set aside time each week to talk with each other.

Communication means listening to information from teens we would rather not hear. Instead of being critical, a parent can keep lines of communication open with words like, "Even though I don't agree with you, thanks for sharing your point of view."

Parents can also use "I"-messages to express their feelings. "I"-messages tell teens where you stand rather than where they need to go. Mom uses an "I"-message when talking to Kent: "It really bothers me when you take my car without asking. I will be happy to let you use it when I don't need it, as long as, I don't have to worry about it being taken without permission."

Give up some control— Many parents make more rules for their teens at a time when there should be fewer rules. Only give your teen rules you can enforce—rules for situations that directly affect you.

♥

GUIDELINES TO REDUCE FAMILY STRESS
• Respect each other's needs
• Encourage an open relationship
• Give up some control
• Set rules only for situations that directly affect you

75

Does Repeating a Grade Ever Work?

"MY SON'S TEACHER SAYS HE NEEDS TO REPEAT HIS GRADE NEXT YEAR. I want him to do well in school, but this has to be a terrible blow to his self-confidence. What do I do?"

I hear this question over and over each spring. It's a parent's expression of frustration and anger about the fact that their child's achievement problems have not been solved. It's a time of shattered dreams. It's also time for some very serious decision making for both school personnel and parents.

The decision to retain a student is a decision that must not be made lightly. The fallout from this decision can have a lasting impact on the child.

Punishment Is Tempting

The temptation is often to do something to the child to show that he/she is not going to get away with poor school performance. Retention, and/or threats of retention, are often the first things that come to mind.

Rather than doling out punishment or threats, time can be better spent discovering the root causes behind a child's lack of success in school. Professionals have just recently discovered that 97% of the children who avoid their schoolwork, have self-concept problems.

When to Retain?

1. Identify the root causes— Until the root causes of a child's academic problems are found, retention will not only be fruitless, it will be permanently damaging. Identifying the root causes of the problem is something that requires the cooperation of both teacher and parent. It cannot be done by either teacher or parent alone, since it requires looking at

family patterns and the reactions of the child at school. Caution! Do not consider retention until this first step has been achieved.

2. Create a plan for success— Once the root cause has been identified, a plan can be developed. Unless a solid plan that indicates a 90–100% chance of success exists, retention not only will be a wasted effort, but may be permanently damaging. This plan usually includes changes at home, strong cooperation between school and home, some individual counseling for the child, as well as, different teaching and relationship strategies at school. Do not consider retention until this step has been achieved.

3. Administer "Light's Retention Scale"— H. Wayne Light, Ph.D., discovered there are 19 different aspects of a child's life that need to be considered before deciding to use retention. He has developed a scale that is very helpful when parents and professionals work together to make the retention decision.

4. Provide effective counseling— It is important that child, parent, and teacher each feels good about retention. If any one of these does not, it is doomed. It is especially important for the youngster to feel good about this decision. Children who are not adequately and effectively helped with their beliefs about retention, usually suffer long-term self-concept problems, resulting in additional learning problems as the years go on.

Retention is rarely a solution for underachievement problems. It is effective only when all the following questions can be answered with a resounding "yes."

1. Have the root causes of the problem been discovered?
2. Has an effective plan of treatment been developed and accepted by both the professionals and the parents?
3. Does the Light's Retention Scale indicate the child is a good candidate for retention?
4. Does the child feel good about the retention?
5. Do the parents feel good about the retention?
6. Does the school feel good about the retention?

If any one of these questions receives a negative answer, forget about retention until all six questions receive a resounding *"yes."*

Do not retain a child unless you have an effective plan for treating the underlying cause of the problem

76

"Finish Your Beets!" Avoiding Struggles Around Food

I FEEL SADDER ABOUT FAMILY DISAGREEMENTS AROUND FOOD than any other single issue. Such fights are generally unnecessary and can easily be prevented. I will give you four guidelines on handling food, but first I want to explore some important thoughts about food.

There are many examples of the connection between food and love. We say, "I love you, Sweetheart," or, "You're the frosting on my cake." Yet, when people fight around food, the important connection between love and food is lost.

Too many of us eat in a rush. In the old days, families would sit and talk, recapping the day, spinning yarns, enjoying each other. We ought to be relaxed at meal times, showing love and affection around food.

GUIDELINE 1:
Saying, "Try it, you'll like it," is not helpful and generally not true— People's tastes change naturally with age, not through learning. Children and adults have taste buds of differing sensitivity. One doesn't find the average child lapping up eggplant, some cheeses, or sweetbreads. About one-fourth of all adults remember, as children, not being able to stomach the feel of tapioca in their mouths. To a child, it simply feels "gushy," or " icky." I remember my grandfather telling me, as a child, to put a pill, "way in the back of your mouth so you won't taste it." I tried it. Was I ever surprised! I thought, "My grandpa lied! He thought I wouldn't taste it." Not only do children's and adult's taste buds differ in sensitivity, but placement of primary taste also changes as a child grows older. Children go around looking like chipmunks with

gumballs jammed back into their jaw because that's where they taste food. In contrast, adults taste most acutely on the tip of the tongue.

GUIDELINE 2:

Give information about food before prohibitions and orders— For instance, it might be wise to say, "When kids eat so little before dessert and then eat a lot of sweets, they don't get much vitamin D. Their bones turn soft. You could probably still walk, Jake, without collapsing, but I'm sure glad I eat good stuff before I layer it with sugar or I might be pretty weak myself!" Sometimes parents may have to use rules around food. However, it is important to remember that, as our children grow older, we will never, but never, be able to control what they put into their mouths. Children need to learn to make their own good rules about what they eat.

GUIDELINE 3:

Anger and frustration around food issues almost always make the problem worse— I'll never forget the mother who brought her child to see me. Sitting in the waiting room, while I saw his mother, the child bought a soda. When his mother finished her part of the session, she spied him sipping his soda, while quietly reading a magazine. Mom became hysterical. She wailed, "He'll become hyper, he'll become hyper." The boy started shaking. I started shaking. Mom was shaking. We were all hyper. Contrast this with the parent who says, "Wow! You didn't eat any sweets until dinner time! I bet you're proud of yourself! That's hard to do!"

GUIDELINE 4 :

Use natural consequences for food fads and other food problems only if encouragement and talking things over has not worked— Parents can use consequences such as: "If all you want to eat is hamburger, you'll probably need to fix it yourself." Or, "I'll pay half for all the sugar-coated cereals you want. If you want them bad enough to earn the other half of what they cost, great!" Most of us eat what we need. Obesity and weight problems correlate most with genetics. Keeping this in mind, we can come to see that many food fights with our children are avoidable and unnecessary.

We ought to be relaxed at meal times,
showing love and affection around food

77

Is Criticism Ever Constructive?

I KNOW A MAN WHO MET A KILLER—HIMSELF. He had systematically killed the spirit of someone he loved the most, his own son. What hurt this man the most was that he had done it out of his love and his desire that his son grow up with none of the flaws he saw in himself. He discovered that he had killed his son's spirit, not on purpose, but with love and criticism. Now, this dad doesn't know how to go back and change what he did. His grown son is seeing a therapist to try to rebuild his shattered self-confidence and attempt to discover happiness. Sadly, he has become the same kind of critic he once despised his father for being.

It's interesting that parents who are critical with their children never admit to using criticism. When asked what they want most for their youngsters, these parents say they want them to grow up to be happy adults. Yet, children who live under criticism grow up to be both critical and chronically unhappy. Isn't this ironic?

As one extremely critical parent said to me, "I don't criticize my daughter. I guide her! She must know what she's doing wrong, so she doesn't continue to make the same mistakes."

If you could spy into this home, you would hear Mom's constant scolding about how the daughter washes her face, puts on a blouse that does not match and talks too loudly during breakfast. She even criticizes the quality of the child's kiss as she leaves for school. She humiliates her daughter in front of her friends with reprimands. "Your computer disks are all over the floor! Those disks are expensive. Maybe if you had to pay for these things, you'd be a little more care-ful!" She marches the child into the house right in front of her friends.

Mom describes this approach as guiding her child. Professionals have different terms for her so-called guidance. These include attacking, nagging, humiliation, faultfinding, ridicule, rejection, and criticism.

Regardless of the terms we use to describe this style of parenting, the results are the same—deadly. These results don't show up for years. Children grow up to become less and less confident. They even become their own best critics. Their spirits are slowly eroded away.

I have a friend who grew up this way. He has never found true happiness. He says he always has been afraid to try things that appeal to him for fear he won't do them right. Even though the person who criticized him so severely is no longer living, the voices are still in his mind—"It's no longer my dad that does the criticizing," he says. "I have taken over that job for myself. I constantly remind myself of my inadequacies. I spend much more time paying attention to what I do wrong, than what I do right."

This man has another regret. "The sad part of this, is that I find myself criticizing my own children the same way my dad ragged on me. The more unhappy I get, the more I try to correct my kids so they don't grow up just like me. I've become part of a vicious circle."

Try to see your children as children, not as small adults. They will learn by making mistakes when, and if, they are allowed to experience the consequences of these mistakes. Be sad for them as they live with these consequences. Bite your tongue when you want to tell them what they did wrong. They can figure that out for themselves. Bite your tongue when you have impatient words that indicate they don't measure up.

Do yourself a favor. Do your children a favor. Focus upon the things they do well. Call these things to their attention 10 times as often as you talk about the things they don't do well. You will be rewarded with children who treat you well, notice your strengths instead of your faults, and grow up to be happy adults, who have broken the criticism cycle.

❤

Do yourself a favor—do your children a favor—
remember that youngsters don't learn by being corrected,
they learn through example and modeling

78

Success with an ADHD Child

"I CAN'T GET MY SON TO BE RESPONSIBLE FOR ANYTHING, especially his schoolwork. He can't remember a thing. He's driving me insane!" I bet you recognize the person saying this as the parent of a child who's been diagnosed as having attention deficit hyperactive disorder, or ADHD for short.

Parents of ADHD children are among the most frustrated parents I have ever known. It doesn't help that a common belief about children who suffer from ADHD says that they can't remember, and can't concentrate, for any prolonged period of time. Fortunately, many of the recent discoveries about ADHD show that these children can be motivated to remember, concentrate, and learn from the consequences of their mistakes. They often just have more difficulty in these areas than other children.

Since drug therapy alone is usually not successful with these children, the solution to this problem often involves a combination of drug therapy and changes in the way parents work with their children. These changes include a willingness and determination on the part of parents to work on changing only one behavior at a time. This shows the child that the parents can, and will, be successful in expecting responsible behavior. When this approach is used, a ripple effect takes place. Parents who are willing to focus most of their energy on helping the child change only one behavior at a time, find success quicker with each new behavior that they tackle.

Parents who master the four steps explained below, will see dramatic changes. Each step will be easier than the last. It is essential, however, that parents move to the next step only after total mastery of the previous step. This is the secret to success in this process.

STEP ONE: The child learns to complete chores without reminders— Roger must believe that his parents think successful completion of chores is the only important thing in the world. To

accomplish this, the parents say, "Your chores are important. We expect you to do them, without reminders, before your next meal. Your next meal may come today, tomorrow, or Saturday. You decide."

It works best to start this step with Roger at a time close to the dinner hour so that the consequence for not remembering the chores is available in a timely fashion. Most children will argue, bargain, and manipulate at this point. It is crucial that the parent not give in. Be prepared to say over and over, "I'm sure this doesn't feel fair, and you will eat when the chores are done." Remember there are to be no reminders, reasoning, or arguing with the child about the fairness of the situation.

STEP TWO: The child learns to go to time-out— "Off to your room, dear. Please return when you can be sweet. Thank you." In this second step, Roger learns that his parents mean business when sending him to time out. Once more, work on only this problem until there is success. Some parents have seen success hiring an older neighborhood child to keep their youngster in his room. It is even better when the child pays for this service with either his allowance or a toy.

STEP THREE: The child learns to have only "good minutes" in the classroom— In this step, Roger's parents tell him that school and learning are privileges. The parents, and Roger, meet with his teacher and agree that Roger is to learn to sit in class without bothering other students or the teacher. The parents back the teacher by saying, "If Roger cannot go to time-out in a pleasant way, call this phone number and someone will pick him up and take him home. We will not complain or lecture him. However, he will do some chores to make up for the inconvenience."

STEP FOUR: The child completes classroom assignments— This step requires a fool proof communication system between teacher and parent. At this point, the parents say to Roger, "Now you are ready to start doing your school assignments. We expect them to be done at school. Any assignments, not completed at school, will be supervised at home. Each supervised assignment will require a payment, on your part, of one chore."

Many parents have been successful treating attention deficit hyperactive disorder with this method. It is also helpful to obtain the advice of a pediatrician regarding how drug therapy may make this process more workable.

❤

ADHD children can be motivated to remember, concentrate, and learn from the consequences of their mistakes

79

One Parent Playing the Role of Two

RAISING CHILDREN IS A CHALLENGE TO MOST PARENTS, but it can be overwhelming to those who try to play the role of both Mom and Dad.

Although single parents are in sharp contrast to the traditional families of our parent's generation, today's single parents are no longer unique. However, they do face special difficulties.

Finding Enough Time

Juggling a household, a job (sometimes two jobs), and the needs of their children is the hardest challenge for single parents. Most are frustrated by their lack of time and feelings of guilt. They feel bad about not spending enough time with their children, not making time for themselves, and the impact of their divorce on their family.

An open and honest attitude about their situation can foster a healthy parent-child relationship. A single parent says to Erica, "I'm in a real tough spot. I'd love to spend more time with you, but it's just not possible right now. How do you think we can make the best of our time together?"

When parents silently bury their feelings, their guilt rubs off onto their children. If parents come through with the attitude, "Oh, you poor kids, it's sad how much I have to work to support us," children will become resentful and play on their parents' guilt. It's much healthier to say, "Aren't we lucky that I have a good job so we can have enough clothes and food? Although it's sometimes hard on us, we have lots to be thankful for." By turning the situation into a positive, children often rise to the occasion with their support.

Respect

Respect is sometimes more difficult for single parents who, tired and overburdened with responsibilities, might find it easier to yell at their children at the end of a hard day. We earn respect by making sure we communicate with our children in a respectful manner, and vice versa.

In the following example, Mom earns Ritchie's respect by expressing her feelings in a calm manner: "I don't feel like being around you today, if you're going to talk rudely. Why don't you go some place for a while—on a walk or to your room. You're welcome back when you decide to talk nicely." In this case, Mom made it clear that she wouldn't tolerate disrespectful behavior. She also modeled to Ritchie how to take good care of herself, as opposed to, criticizing his behavior. In doing so, she reduced a lot of personal stress, time, and effort. This mother is a very effective single parent.

❤

A single parent can be very effective

80

When Grandparents Should Act

GRANDPA AND GRANDMA WERE VISITING, and it was Frankie's bedtime. "Aw, Mom, Grandpa and Grandma are here, and I want to stay up later. There's no school tomorrow anyway, and I can sleep in." Grandma leaped in on his behalf, "It's okay, Mary, just let him stay up. After all, we only get to visit here once in a blue moon."

Although Mary, Frankie's mother, was in the driver's seat, Grandma was grabbing the steering wheel. Grandparents shouldn't grab steering wheels from the passenger side, but sometimes they may serve as navigators, or take a turn behind the wheel. There are four scenarios in which grandparents, or other adults, get involved in driving—four kinds of occasions when they set policy with children.

1. When a child's behavior directly affects the grandparent— During that same visit, Frankie took his grandfather's electric shaver from his suitcase and tried it out. Having no facial hair, he experimented on his arms, then left the hair-filled shaver on the floor of his room.

When Grandpa searched for, and finally found, his shaver the next morning, he said to Frankie, "My suitcase is private territory, and I don't like people using my shaver, especially without asking. I'm ready to shave, and I need a clean shaver." After explaining the cleaning procedure, Grandpa said, "When it's clean, please knock on the bathroom door and return it to me. Thanks, bud."

2. When a child's behavior violates Grandpa and Grandma's house rules— On home turf, grandparents have the right to set the standards. My wife and I are less lenient about chil-

dren's clutter and mess than our adult children are. When our grandchildren visit, they adjust to our house rules.

Sometimes grandchildren may protest a rule saying, "At home we don't have to put things away." It's not necessary to criticize their parents, or defend your reason for your standards. A grandparent can simply say, "That's fine, and you're at Grandma's house now. At Grandma's house, we go by Grandma's rules. At your parent's house, we go by their rules."

3. When parents are not present— In many instances, when parents are not present, grandparents become the parent figure, and they need to set limits for behavior and respond to misbehavior.

Grandpa Vic took his five-year-old grandson, Frankie, shopping. After they left a department store, Vic noticed Frankie's pockets were bulging and saw a candy bar he had not purchased in each. "What's in your pocket, Frankie?" he asked. "Candy bars. I found them lying there," Frankie said. "When you find something in a store, it belongs to the store," said Vic. "If you take it, that's really sad, because stealing is not a good thing to do."

"We need to find the owner so you can give them back, explain what you did, and tell him or her you are sorry." When they found the manager, Vic let Frankie do the talking. Frankie's voice quivered and his eyes were wet, but he took responsibility for his action. "I took these candy bars, and I am very sorry," he told the manager.

When Vic returned Frankie home that day, he said nothing until Frankie had gone out to the swing set. Then he briefly told Frankie's parents what had happened. Because Vic had been alone with Frankie, he had been responsible for discipline.

4. If a parent has agreed that a grandparent may take action— Good grandparenting, when relating to your adult children, lies in being overt and up front rather than covert and devious. Some parents may respond by saying, "Sure, fine. If you see something that bothers you, speak up!" Others may say, "If you want to follow up, or back up, something I say, that's fine, but I'd rather not have you say something before I do." Or, a parent might respond, "No, if something needs to be said when we are all together, I will say it." Their answer is rooted

in their sense of their nuclear family boundaries, and grandparents do well to respect those boundaries.

Grandparents and parents who struggle with these boundaries may even set up an agreed signal. Grandpa may say, "I really don't have a clear sense of when you feel I'm invading your parental territory, so when you feel that's happening, please tug on your right earlobe, and I will back off."

❤

Good grandparents are overt and up front,
rather than covert and devious

Chapter Nine

81

Setting Limits

CHILDREN NEED FIRM LIMITS. Limits are the foundation of security. Children lucky enough to have limits placed on them in loving ways, are then secure enough to develop self-confidence. These children are easier to teach, spend less time acting out, and usually get along well with other children and adults.

I have seen many children misbehave in a variety of ways, in desperate attempts to get their parents to set limits. It is almost as if they were trying to say, "Don't you love me? How bad do I have to act before you will set some limits for me?"

Setting firm limits is a gift of love. The problem is that we often find setting limits difficult. Children fight the limits to see if they are firm enough to provide security. They test us by saying that we are mean or that we don't love them. It is easy to become confused at this point and change the limits. That is the last thing children really need.

Avoid giving orders. Orders do not set limits; they encourage battles. Consider the following order: "I've called you to dinner three times already! You get in here and eat your dinner!" It encourages the child to be late just to test the limits.

Try instead, "I'm serving dinner in five minutes. Hope you join us. If not, breakfast will be at the regular time." This leaves the youngster with much more to think about, such as, "It doesn't sound as if Mom is going to be serving a special meal for me if I'm late." Most parents are pleasantly surprised at the results when they describe what they plan to do, instead of telling the child what he/she has to do.

Avoid orders— "You're not going to talk to me like that in my own house!" *(fighting words)*

Try stating what you are willing to do— "I'd be willing to listen to you about that when your voice is as soft as mine." *(thinking words)*

Avoid telling what you won't do— "I'm not giving you any more allowance just because you wasted yours already!" *(fighting words)*

Try stating what you will do— "Don't worry sweetie. You'll have some money when your usual allowance comes on Saturday." *(thinking words)*

Limits are often set by offering choices. A mother, getting ready to go shopping, sets limits through choices. "Would you rather go shopping with me and keep your hands to yourself, or would you rather take some of your allowance money and hire a sitter to stay with you at home?" I have an idea that if the children don't behave in the store this week, they will be hiring their own sitter next time, and Mom will enjoy her shopping.

❤

Set limits using "thinking words" instead of "fighting words"

82

Party-Time and Your Adolescents

MANY TEENS DREAM ABOUT THE FUN PARTIES they'll have when their parents are away, or even those they'll attend. And while they dream, their parents try to think of ways to restrict their party activities, often with unsuccessful results. The following guidelines can be helpful to parents faced with these kinds of situations:

RULE 1:

Never give an order you can't enforce— Parents often give orders that backfire. This is because the teens who need orders, also disobey them, while those who follow them probably don't need them!

It's far more effective to say, "I don't want you to have a party while we're away," or "I'm hoping you'll avoid parties where drugs are present." Then, if your teen disobeys your expectations, you have not lost as much as if your teen disobeys a direct order.

RULE 2:

Wise parents get serious, not angry, about party behavior— While some parents get angry at their teen's behavior, wise parents get serious by letting consequences unfold.

The following illustrates this point:

When John's parents were gone, he held a party that resulted in damage to the family's new stereo system. In a calm manner, John's father let him know that repairs were totally his responsibility. After several time-consuming trips to the repair shop and a $370 bill, John appeared less interested in being a host. "Parties can be real expensive," he said.

Rule 3:

Let your teen know you will help if needed— Wise parents keep lines of communication open, without rescuing. They listen (even to information they don't want to hear), remain loving, and never confuse acceptance of party behavior with its approval.

Rule 4:

Prohibit attendance at parties only when a teen will obey and truly can't cope— Make sure both criteria of this rule are met before prohibiting your teen from going to a party.

    Example: Paul, despite his father's warning, attended a party where alcohol was served. His father had decided that, no matter what happened, Paul would be able to cope. Later, after breaking up the party, police contacted Paul's father, asking him to pick up his son. Despite accusations of negligence, he refused. Instead, Paul spent the night in detention learning some valuable lessons: "I should have listened to my dad," and "I can handle detention once, but never again!"

Rule 5:

Require your teen to tell you where he or she is and when he or she will return— Why should teens let us know where they are going and when they'll return? Most parents answer, "Because we worry!" But that response usually leads to even less responsible behavior by teens. Parents do need to know their teens' where-abouts—because *they promise not to worry!*

❤

Wise Parents Help without Rescuing

83

Allowances

"KIDS LEARN MORE ABOUT USING MONEY WISELY when we allow them to feel the consequences of using it unwisely." This is a direct quote from one of Jim Fay's parenting tapes. He often talks about the wisdom of giving children weekly allowances. Allowances can serve many purposes.

Many parents find it helpful to provide an allowance for children, once they reach the age of five or six. The money comes each week, on the same day, in an envelope which reads, "From Mom and Dad with Love." The amount of the allowance is not as important as consistently following the rules.

Rule number one is that the child does not earn the money. Jim Fay warns that children should not be paid to do their chores. Being paid for chores robs a child of the dignity of holding up his or her fair share of the family workload. Children who do not have to do this can often become hard to live with during their teenage years.

Rule number two says that the child is allowed to spend, save, or waste the money as he or she sees fit. The catch here is that once the money is gone, there is no more until the next "payday." When Sally says, "I want some bubble gum, but I don't have any money," the best parental reply is, "That's sad, but don't worry. There will be more on Saturday." This is a wonderful opportunity for Sally to learn from her mistakes, and for the parent to make a very easy decision.

Rule number three states we never take away money when our children forget chores. That may sound suspicious, but Jim reminds

us that instead of taking the money away, we should allow children to pay someone else to do their chores. He says, children should go first class anytime *they* can afford it. An allowance gives them a chance to be just like adults, and to hire others to do what they forget or don't like to do.

When Roger forgets to mow the lawn, a parent can then say, "No problem, Roger. I'm sure you can hire your little sister to do it. Why don't you check to see how much she will charge. I'm sure your allowance will cover that. If you run into a problem, I'm always looking for a part-time job, but you might want to remember that I charge adult wages."

The allowance also makes it possible for parents to say, "Would you rather clean up your room, or hire me to do it for you?" Questions like these cause children to be so busy thinking, that they have less time to be angry.

♥

RULES FOR ALLOWANCES
1. The child does not earn the allowance.
2. We never take it away.
3. No restrictions on its use.
4. It comes on the same day of each week.
5. Once it's gone, it's gone!

84

When Our Children Really Think!

DON'T BE SURPRISED IF YOUR 13-YEAR-OLD replaces her play-by-play description of her day with angry outbursts. What is happening is a gradual, almost magical, shift in the way your child thinks. Up until the early teens, a child thinks immaturely, with little ability to conceptualize. Around age 13, a young person begins to think like an adult.

Jean Piaget, the famous Swiss psychologist, studied the development of thinking in children. He referred to the thinking of elementary and early junior high schoolers as "concrete operations," and named mature thinking "formal operations." Piaget found that mature thinking automatically results from growing up and can neither be hurried, nor delayed, by either parents or the educational system.

New Ways of Relating

As children try to adjust to "formal operations" type thinking and begin to question their parents' behavior, they often display their new thinking style through anger, outbursts, and retorts.

For the first time, they can truly judge their own ability to handle difficult situations, and for the first time, their judgment on issues affecting their lives may be better than that of their parents! This new ability to think is at the heart of many parent/child misunderstandings.

You may notice some of the following changes in your child as he or she moves into adult-type thinking:

1. Parents no longer hear long and detail-packed stories of movies, school, or other activities.

2. For the first time, your child understands the meaning of parables and sayings such as, "People who live in glass houses shouldn't throw stones."

3. Children begin to understand political cartoons on a deeper level, rather than just laughing about a character's big nose or humorous appearance.

4. No longer do our children ask questions whose answers seem obvious. No longer do parents hear, "I don't get it, Mom."

5. Young people begin to question, for the first time, whether or not the end justifies the means.

6. Children no longer automatically buy into their parents' value systems just because they love their parents.

7. Young people begin to both question, and comment, on their parents' behavior from a more objective perspective.

Let Them Take Flight!

While parents may find some of these changes confusing, and at times disruptive, it helps to understand that they are a natural and important part of a child's development. You can expect this shift toward conceptual adult thinking to take place over a period of about six months.

Parents, who have raised responsible children, can welcome this change as a major step in their child's development into adulthood. They can also recognize it as a time to back off, let their children unfold their newly found cerebral wings, and take flight. They'll be equipped to leave the nest when it's time.

♥

The gift of thinking allows a child to grow

85

Survival Skills for the Real World

ARE KIDS FACING MORE LIFE AND DEATH DECISIONS THAN EVER? Are they being challenged, at earlier ages than before, with scarier choices about drugs, alcohol, sex, and violence? Clearly, most children are growing up in a much more challenging world than we ever imagined. And, the consequences of mistakes are more serious than ever!

Of great concern is the fact that many children are not being equipped with the survival skills necessary for making wise decisions about these pressures. More and more kids seem to believe that bad things can't really happen until after their second or third poor decision. What do I mean? Perhaps an example will better illustrate this point.

Not long ago, I took my son to the movies. As we sat through the multitude of previews and ads for giant sized butter-flavored popcorn, I noticed two boys sitting near the front, throwing ice. Their parents were seated about three rows behind them. Mom walked up to them and said something like, "You stop that. I mean it. That's one."

A minute or two later, the ice once again began to sail. This time dad approached them and said very loudly, "Mom told you to stop that. Now that's two."

Soon the popcorn began to fly. Dad rushed back down to them and said, "Stop that. If you keep doing that we're going to have to leave!"

Finally, after three or four warnings, these parents put some action behind their threats and took the kids home. What happens

when we give children two or three warnings before we deliver a consequence? We condition them to believe that they can always make at least two poor decisions before anything unfortunate happens. Does this give kids a strong defense against peer pressure? Absolutely not! Why? Because down deep they start to develop "tapes" inside of their heads that say things like, "I can smoke crack (or have sex, drink and drive, carry a gun, and so on) at least two times before anything bad happens."

I had a friend in high school with this view. His parents had always warned him at least three times before they actually followed-through. He lived for a short while believing that nothing bad could happen, unless he'd been warned at least twice. Then he died the first time he went to a party, got drunk, and tried to drive home in a mountain snowstorm.

Love and Logic parents know that kids need to understand bad things can happen after the first poor decision—without repeated warnings. How do they teach this? They set limits once, and follow-through with meaningful consequences rather than more warnings. What does this look like in the movie theatre? Mom or dad walks over and whispers, "Are you guys going to be able to behave, or do we need to go?" If the boys act-up again, mom and dad don't lecture or warn. Instead, they say something like, "How sad. We're going home now. By the way, how are you guys going to pay us for the money we spent on tickets, soda, and popcorn? You can tell us later. Try not to worry about it."

❤

Set limits once, then follow-through with meaningful consequences

86

When Substance Abuse Threatens

SUBSTANCE OR DRUG ABUSE IS A COMMON AND COMPLEX PROBLEM. Unfortunately, many teens experiment with drugs at some point. Fortunately, most do not go on to use or abuse drugs.

The following are eight important facts about substance abuse:

1. Alcohol is the most commonly-abused substance— Alcohol and nicotine cause far more deaths than any illegal substance. Adults are the largest abusers of both.

2. Nicotine is linked to the most deaths— Parents who smoke, need to be up front with their children by admitting their addiction is seriously hurting their health.

3. Nicotine is the most addicting substance— Nicotine is now believed to be even more addicting than cocaine. Let teens know that manufacturers are counting on them just trying cigarettes so they'll be hooked!

4. Some types of drug use are more dangerous than others— Experimentation, drug use, and drug abuse are three types of drug involvement. Although most who experiment do not go on to abuse drugs, parents must take a hard line against any type of drug use— without demonstrating anger.

5. Cocaine and other drugs are being distributed and used by elementary school children in all socioeconomic groups throughout the country— Parents need to provide their children

with solid information on drugs. They are generally interested, as long as articles and material are factual.

6. A loving and open parent/child relationship is the best insurance against drug abuse— Drug use/abuse does not occur in a vacuum, but is a sign of a poor parent/child relationship. Strong bonds of love and open communication are the best ways to prevent the problem.

Because much drug use is a sign of rebellion, orders are bound to make the problem worse. Instead, as difficult as it may be, opinions and consequences should be given without anger.

7. Learn how to talk to your teens about drug abuse— Let your teens know that parents are accessories to a crime when illegal drugs are in the home. You will simply call the police. The same applies to drinking and driving. Statements about taking care of ourselves, and not being accessories to a crime, are much more effective than lecturing about what's good for them! Thoughtful parents let their teenagers know that drug users pretty much have to deal with the law on their own!

8. Learn the signs of drug abuse, while understanding that other problems may mimic drug abuse— Signs can include a sudden drop in school grades, or change in friendships. Changes in the size of the eye pupil may indicate acute drug use, while marijuana use can cause a reddening of the eye conjunctiva. Amphetamine use may cause teens to act like they have a chip on their shoulder or are paranoid. Drug highs may be followed by depression.

❤

ANGER simply makes drug abuse more likely!
OPEN, loving relationships with our teens are
the best insurance against drug abuse

87

Don't Shoot the Teacher!

SOME CHILDREN ARE PRECONDITIONED TO BE UNDERACHIEVERS before they ever enter a school. The teachers and parents of these children often spend years of frustration trying to get these youngsters to achieve their potential. They are often faced with discouragement and disappointment as they watch bright children, who seem to want to achieve, but just can't seem to put out the effort necessary for success. It is almost as if these children have learned to avoid the very things they need, in order to be successful learners.

It is so easy to blame the school. However, there are many learning related problems that do not start in the school, and cannot be cured by having more discipline, more understanding teachers, or more time spent teaching the basics.

Consider the following situation in which one parent had to struggle for everything she got as a youngster. As an adult she is dedicated to making sure her child does not have to experience the same pain. At the same time, her husband believes it is best for children to earn what they get. This provides the potential for a family pattern that can create an underachieving child.

The child in this family soon learns how to get what he wants. "Daddy, I need some more money. My allowance ran out." Father will answer, "That's sad. You'll have to wait until Saturday for your regular allowance."

The youngster goes to Mother with, "Mom, look how mean Daddy is!" Mother, who is dedicated to making sure the child experiences no pain, finds herself saying, "Now, now. Don't worry. Daddy's just tired and doesn't understand. I'll get you some money, but be sure you don't tell Daddy."

Mother is hoping to show that she is a loving friend. The sad truth is that the foundation for underachievement has just been laid. Yes, the child may see Mother as loving; but, a devastating lesson has just been learned: you get what you want through manipulation, not through effort.

This attitude may be firmly in place by the time the child goes to school. You can guess what the youngster thinks when the teacher says, "Here is some schoolwork to do, it will take some effort." This poor child thinks, "No! Effort is not the way you get what you want. There is an easier way."

It will not be long before this student tries to defend poor grades by saying, "Look how mean the teacher is. She just doesn't understand." This seems so sincere that, before long, the student has manipulated both parents into joining with him or her against the school and the teacher. The child now has more power than either the parents or the teacher.

It is not unusual for parents in this situation to be confused, first blaming the school, then blaming the child, and then blaming themselves; all with no success in getting the child to live up to his/her potential. Attempted interventions include daily reports from the teacher, more homework, rewards, punishment, school conferences, labels such as "learning disabled," and special education classes to explain away the problem.

None of these will work because they are not at the root of this youngster's problem. The problem will be solved when the parents discover that they need to have a consistent set of expectations for the child: "We both want the best for you and we both know that it will come from effort, not from manipulating one of us against the other."

❤

Kids Need Consistent Messages about Effort

Talking about Suicide: When Your Teen Needs Help

UNFORTUNATELY, SUICIDE IS ONE OF THE LEADING CAUSES OF DEATH among adolescents. It is a grave problem that parents must take seriously, while recognizing that some suicidal threats are manipulative in nature.

The following points may be helpful for parents faced with this complex problem:

1. It's best not to put the word "suicide" into an adolescent's head. If you have reason to be concerned, or if your teen has indirectly referred to suicide, the thought has probably already entered his or her mind.

2. When talking about suicide, show concern and caring while remaining matter-of-fact. Responses like, "You don't mean that" usually make matters worse.

3. The situation is usually more dangerous if a teenager has already thought of a specific lethal method, and has the means at his or her disposal. Giving away favorite objects is another serious sign.

4. Most authorities believe the risk is higher if depression or suicide runs in the family.

5. Teens at greatest risk are those who usually achieve without struggle. They often expect success to be automatic and, at times when they think they are failing, have difficulty believing struggle will lead to solutions.

Help Your Teen Examine Other Options

When talking to our teens about suicide, the goal is to help them pursue other options. At the same time, a parent must consider other avenues of support, such as counseling, support groups, and, if necessary, hospitalization.

The following is a parent talking to his daughter about suicide in a loving manner:

DAD: "You seem pretty down these days."

KATE: *(sigh)* "I don't want to talk about it . . ."

DAD: "Sometimes things seem so bad, as if there's no way out."

KATE: *(softening)* "Yeah."

DAD: "You've been so unhappy—I wonder if you feel life just isn't worth living."

KATE: *(softer)* "I do, Dad. It's just that everything turns out wrong. I'd probably be better off dead."

DAD: "Are there any other solutions?"

KATE: "I probably wouldn't do it. I'm too chicken . . ."

DAD: "When I'm feeling really down, it always helps me to talk to someone else."

KATE: "Like a shrink?"

DAD: "Maybe. The nice thing about seeing a therapist is you can always quit if things don't seem better. I know, because I've been there. I hope you'll think about finding someone to talk with."

KATE: "I will, Dad. Thanks."

During this conversation, Kate's dad never becomes defensive. Instead, he stays with her feelings, and lets her know what works for him when he is down. He does not force Kate into a decision. If he did, she might say "no." If he allows her to give it some thought, she might say "yes."

In summary, explore possibilities with your teen in a loving, calm, and receptive manner, without moralizing or downplaying the problem. In addition, mobilize support when necessary.

❤

Recognize When Your Teen Is in Danger

89

Bossy Children

IS IT ANY WONDER THAT BOSSY PARENTS OFTEN HAVE BOSSY CHILDREN? Parents who order their youngsters around like boot-camp recruits end up with children who want to be drill sergeants.

However, it's not always the parents who are at fault. Even non-bossy moms and dads have bossy youngsters, on occasion. Oftentimes, these children are simply addicted to having their own way. Bossing others is one way to accomplish that goal.

Occasionally, these control-conscious children will even turn their demanding mouths on their parents. One way to handle this is to be prepared with a well-rehearsed one-liner.

When children become bossy, our first response is a nice, extended smile. This unexpected turn of events gives them time to think, to wonder what in the world is going on. Then, quietly, we say, "Nice try, Sarah. What do you think happens in this family when people get real bossy? Does it help or not? Please don't answer that now. Just give it some thought." Then we break eye contact and walk away.

The behavior is dealt with in an unemotional and straightforward manner. We deal with bossy children without emotion because emotion just gives them ammunition to turn on us. Parents who lay into their children with, "Don't you dare order me around!" suddenly find themselves hooked into a power struggle.

However, when children begin to boss other kids, the problem becomes the child's, not the parent's:

MOM: "Sarah, I notice that you're kind of bossy with your friends. Do you ever worry about losing their friendship because of bossiness?

SARAH: "Aw, they'd still be my friends."
MOM: "Well, good luck. I'll be interested to see how it works out."

Chances are somewhere along the line it won't work out well. The real world will drive the lesson home—being bossy can cause you to lose friends in a hurry. Other kids happily provide learning experiences for bossy kids like Sarah.

Then, when Sarah returns to Mom's side with her problem, Mom should express the sadness of a true friend:

MOM: "Oh, so that really didn't work out?"
SARAH: "No."
MOM: "That's sad. What do you suppose you'll do to get your friends back?"
SARAH: "I don't know."
MOM: "If you would like me to share some ideas with you, let me know, and I'll be glad to talk with you about it. If anyone will give it some thought, I'm sure it will be you."

Bossing our kids around by telling them not to be so bossy only perpetuates the problem, and the bossiness will continue. Children find their own solutions to this problem when parents keep the burden of the problem on the child's shoulders and are nearby with a word of advice. Remember, our advice is only heard when it has been requested.

❤

Children become bossy only when they know it works

90

Five Secrets for Success with Teens

PSYCHIATRIST FOSTER W. CLINE, M.D., offers the following guidelines for parents of teens. While they won't guarantee trouble-free relationships, over time, they can help parents and teens more fully enjoy each other.

1. Give as few rules as possible— As children grow older, they need fewer, not more rules. An unhappy 16-year-old exclaimed, "When I was little, I didn't have to let my parents know where I was every minute." The parents of this girl were making a typical mistake. When she curved out, they clamped down!

2. Give your teenagers rules and orders that you can enforce— Parents are left powerless when they make rules that cannot be enforced. This typically happens when a teen is grounded and refuses to follow the order. Grounding is usually an ineffective consequence. The only rules we can "force" a teen to follow are those that directly affect us. A rule that forbids marijuana smoking, for example, may be disregarded, but a rule that forbids marijuana on the premises will be followed.

3. Keep the lines of communication open— This is often difficult to put into practice. Our children will talk to us when we follow the example of a good therapist. A therapist listens carefully and makes absolutely sure he or she understands the child. A therapist rarely gives orders, and always lets the child make decisions. Finally,

a therapist gives the child a strong message that says, "I may not think what you're doing is great, but, as a person, you're all right."

4. Encourage adolescents to show their autonomy by being different— Healthy teens express their individuality in nondestructive ways. For example, some boys wear a single earring. When parents get upset, it's just what the teen wants, since he is trying hard to prove he is different. Most changes in appearance are not self-destructive. If the teenager is irresponsible, negative, or angry, there are more important problems to worry about.

5. Keep life consequential for the adolescent— Wise parents make sure problem behavior affects their teens directly. Then, they express empathy, instead of anger. Here are some ways this can be done:

• Wise parents pay for "good guy" auto insurance. Teens pay the difference when their insurance increases because of their irresponsible behavior.

• Wise parents do not support illegal behavior by bailing their children out of detention or paying attorney fees!

• Wise parents expect their teens to do chores, treat them with respect, and maintain average grades. Other than that, teens' lives should be their own. Loving parents, with only a few essential rules, have the right to ask their teens to find a different place to live when they refuse to follow guidelines.

• Wise parents always leave the door open for their teens to return, as long as their children put into writing the expectations and rules they will follow. Without a written agreement, another disruption almost always occurs.

❤

Few rules and open communication lines equal more
enjoyment for teens and parents

Chapter Ten

91

"But It Worked for My Dad!"

FOSTER W. CLINE, M.D., psychiatrist, and cofounder of Cline/Fay Institute, Inc., describes today's teenagers as "two-year-olds with hormones and wheels." It's no wonder parents question whether they will survive the stressful adolescent years, when their teens act like defiant toddlers determined to get their own way!

Stress Overload

Many of us have spent sleepless nights questioning our own ability to parent. We may ask, "Why is it so much more complicated now, than when my parents raised me?" Today, a different style of parenting is needed to cope with our complex society.

It helps to recognize most young people are under more stress than we were as teens. They must grow up faster, in a competitive world, where the decisions they make about school, careers, friends, and drugs have serious long-term consequences.

As youngsters, we accepted, without question, what our parents told us. We believed they could make us do the things they asked. It's frustrating, then, when our teens constantly question what we tell them and ask of them. They are growing up in a society that encourages them to stand up for their rights as individuals and say, "Hey! I don't have to put up with this!"

Respect Each Other's Needs

Young people today have a great need to establish their independence and identity at an early age. They show this through their actions. Parents, feeling threatened, often respond by pulling the

reins in tighter. This creates an even stronger need for teenagers to assert themselves.

Parents have needs too. They need to feel they are helping their children grow in the best way they know how. *Therefore, it's time to back off, acknowledge your teen's need to grow, and, at the same time, make sure your own needs are being met.*

It may help to say to your teen, "I love you and want to help you become independent and be your own person. I'm also hoping you'll help me meet my need to know you'll take good care of yourself, so I won't be fearful for you."

When parents and teens accept each other's needs, there is usually less stress in their relationship.

Don't Worry

When we worry too much about our ability to parent, the result can be stress overload. Instead, we need to back off and let our teens learn from their own decisions. Keep in mind that worrying is the price you pay in advance for 92% of the things that never happen!

❤

Acknowledge Your Teen's Need to Grow and, at the Same Time, Make Sure Your Own Needs Are Being Met

92

Who Owns the Problem?

THERE ARE PRACTICAL BENEFITS to figuring out who really owns every problem. Psychiatrist, Foster W. Cline, M.D., once commented, "Parents who have trouble figuring out who has the problem, keep child therapists in bread and butter." When parents do not figure out who has the problem, they raise an irresponsible child.

There is a useful concept called "units of concern." Every problem has a given number of units of concern. You can bet nobody wants to carry those units of concern around, least of all the child causing the problem! Most kids would rather have teachers and parents carry units of concern. If the parent insists on worrying about whether a child does his homework, for example, then the child is free to drop that concern.

When parents carry their kids' concerns, it works about as well as trying to solve another nation's concerns. Let us suppose that, on the television news this evening, we see a green Martian. With antennas waving and yellow eyes bulging, the Martian might declare, "Earthlings, you are a very warlike species. You could wipe each other out! From now on, we are not going to let you hurt each other. We're going to step in! The missiles of any nation being fired at another nation will immediately be destroyed. We are doing this because we love you!" Can you imagine the response? You bet. Within fifteen minutes, the U.S. and Russia would both be shooting at the Martians, who would end up saying, "Well, we were only trying to help." It never helps to take on someone else's problem. It just doesn't work.

Tote up your problems— Understanding who has the problem is important. The list of problems that kids directly cause parents is very short. Mainly it covers:

- How the child relates to the parents
- How the child does chores
- What life support systems the child requires from the parent (bread and butter, room and board).

On the other hand, the list of problems that children need to solve for themselves, is very long: getting to school on time, getting to school at all, dropping out of school, being hassled by friends, hassling friends, harassing teachers, being harassed by teachers, and more. Frankly, it's an unending list. Parents who get involved in their kids' problems, can keep themselves busy for a lifetime.

In summary, if everyone figured out, "Who really has this problem?" most problems between nations would be solved quickly. Most battles on the home front would also be solved quickly. Would we be bored!

❤

Solving my children's problems meets my own needs.
Then I feel like a good parent. Allowing them to find their own
solutions meets their needs. Then they learn to problem solve.

93

Mood Swings— Dr. Jekyll or Mr. Hyde?

REMEMBER THE KIND AND GOOD DOCTOR in R. L. Stevenson's story, *The Strange Case of Dr. Jekyll and Mr. Hyde?* Dr. Jekyll discovered drugs that allowed him to transform himself into a vicious, brutal creature named Mr. Hyde, and then back into the kindly Jekyll.

Sometimes our teens seem like modern versions of Jekyll and Hyde. When they're in a particularly bad mood, we may wonder if they have used drugs or are facing some other awful crisis.

The following are some helpful hints to keep in mind:

1. Mood swings are typical in adolescence— During adolescence, there are more body changes than at any other time in life. In a period of about five years, a teen changes from a child to an adult. The intense physical and emotional changes of adolescence are usually responsible for drastic mood swings.

2. Don't interrogate your teen— The worst thing we can do is ask a depressed teen, "What's the matter with you?" or "Why don't you perk up?" To a teen, that's more like a prosecutor launching an attack!

It's better if parents acknowledge what they see, and let the teen know they are available to talk. You might try caring words like, "I wonder if you're kind of hurting right now?" Then see what your teen says. If your teen does not want to talk, back off.

3. Encourage your teen to share feelings— It's okay to ask your teen, "Are you mad at me right now?" or "Have I done something to hurt you?" It helps if our children share their feelings with us.

One father learned a valuable, but difficult, lesson from his son Charlie. Ron and his wife sought counseling for Charlie because he was depressed for a long time. It took many sessions with a therapist to coax Charlie to explain that he thought his dad was mad at him all the time. Charlie finally asked his dad, "Are you mad at me today?" Surprised, Ron answered, "No." Charlie then asked, "Then why are you frowning at me?" Ron answered that he frowns when he thinks hard. He learned from his son that it makes others think he is angry. Ron had thought he had a great relationship with Charlie. However, Charlie had thought for years that his father was mad at him.

4. Most bad moods don't require a counselor— Unless your teen's depression continues over a long period for no apparent reason, there is usually no reason to seek professional counseling. A teen's bad moods may have nothing to do with the parents. If you have approached your teen about the sadness or depression, and it lasts no more than about two weeks, it's usually better to let the matter rest.

❤

The Intense Physical and Emotional Changes of Adolescence
Are Usually Responsible for Mood Swings

94

"And I Mean It!" Making Your Words Gold

HOW MANY TIMES HAVE YOU HEARD A PARENT give an order to a child and then add, "Do you understand me?" Children can't wait to hear a parent talk like this because it means they have reached the end of their rope. The parent has once again reduced his or her authority through hollow, meaningless words.

This happens each time we make statements that can't be enforced, when we tell a child what to do or not do, rather than what we will do.

In cases where parents frequently make unenforceable statements, children learn they do not have to do whatever the parent says or asks. Parental authority is undermined as children test limits, act out, and feel a general lack of control.

Some parents do not have these problems because their word is gold. They understand that they actually have control over themselves and no one else. The art of making enforceable statements involves talking about ourselves and what we will allow, what we will do, or what we will provide. For example:

Unenforceable: "Don't talk to me like that!"
Enforceable: "I'll be glad to listen when your voice is as soft as mine."

Unenforceable: "Study NOW, young man!"
Enforceable: "Feel free to join us for some TV, when you are finished studying."

Unenforceable: "Be nice to each other. Don't fight."

Enforceable: "You're both welcome to be around me, when you're not fighting."

Unenforceable: "As long as you live in this house, you won't be drinking any alcoholic beverages."

Enforceable: "When I no longer have to worry about alcohol use, I'll let you use my car."

Parents who make only those statements that they can and do enforce, raise children who believe their parents mean what they say. Their children seldom test limits.

This technique needs practice. You might try, "Hey, kids, from now on you need to know that I will be giving you dessert when you protect your teeth by brushing." It's much easier to withhold treats than to cram a toothbrush in a child's mouth!

❤

Talk about what you allow—not what your child can or can't do.

95

Curfews

IF THE SUBJECT OF CURFEWS BRINGS TO MIND ENDLESS BATTLES with your teen, here's a new approach to try. Treat the last three years your teen is home as practice for the real world. The fewer the rules, the better. Ideally, those rules should be the same as in the real world.

In the real world, there are only a few dorm rules, and those who live in apartments set their own rules. Don't panic! That doesn't mean a teen has total freedom. Instead, we ask them to begin making their own rules.

Instead of telling your teen when to be home, ask, "Where are you going?" "Where can I reach you?" and "When should I start worrying?"

The teen should set the curfew. It may be different each time, just like in the real world. What we're doing is preparing our teens to live as adults.

Negotiate

Parents can negotiate with their teens on behavior they can both live with. If a teen says he'll be home at 5:00 a.m., that's unacceptable. A parent can say, "I'm not up to worrying that late," and recognize the teen is just testing.

Two-Way Street

An experienced father of five learned to allow his son Don to make the most of his own decisions, including how late he stayed out. His dad made a deal with him: "I won't hassle you, if you let

me know where you are and how to reach you in an emergency. I'll do the same for you, so you'll always know where I am."

This dad learned that curfews are a two-way street. Once he arrived home two hours late to a household of children who were worried sick. From then on, he called if he was going to be late.

Promise Not to Worry

Expressing fear and concern has a lot more impact than expressing anger with teens who stay out late without letting us know where they are. A wise parent lets their teen know they're the type who doesn't worry: "If you're late, and I don't know where you are, I imagine you could be lying on the side of a road. Fifteen minutes could mean the difference between life and death if you need a transfusion. If you agree to always call when you're late, I'll know nothing is wrong."

Anger Doesn't Work

When a teen walks in the door late and is not even sorry, it naturally makes a parent mad. Yelling only makes things worse. Instead, say, "It's lucky for you that I'm angry because I'm not going to talk to you about being late until tomorrow, when I can think better."

As difficult as this is, it helps to remember we can't reason with teens when they're in an emotional state. The words we use when we're emotional, are often the ones we wish we could take back.

It's far more effective to deal with children when they can really hear us; when we're happy and when they're happy.

❤

Replace anger with concern

96

What's a Parent For?

"HOW CAN I BE A GOOD PARENT if I can't make my kid do what I want him to do, when I want him to do it?"

Award-winning educator Jim Fay, found himself discussing this question with the parent of a rebellious 12-year-old. The discussion didn't start with this question. It started with, "Your speech was very interesting, but what do you do with a child who never hears anything you say?"

Jim asked for more information, and the mother said, "It's just like calling a cat. I call him to dinner and he doesn't even flinch. It's like my words go in one ear and out the other. Let me give you an example. I walk up to him when he is playing with his computer and tell him to come to dinner, and he just ignores me."

"What do you do then?" Jim asked.

"Well," she said, "I raise my voice, but he still doesn't pay attention. It seems like I have to get really mad and stern before he knows that I mean business!"

Jim asked, "How does that work?"

"Well, he doesn't show any respect. He just starts in on me with complaints about our being on his back all the time, and it ends up ruining the dinner every night! What do you do?"

Jim suggested a technique some parents use. These parents go to the child and calmly say, "We will be serving dinner for the next 30 minutes. Sure hope you can make it, but if not, we'll be serving breakfast at the regular time."

"I could never do that," she said. "It's not good for him to miss a meal. He needs his nourishment!"

This gave Jim some interesting thoughts about the quality of the nourishment her son gets when he is doing battle with his folks.

Jim asked, "Are you saying that the technique won't work, or are you saying you just can't stand to think of him getting hungry during the night?"

With this she went on to explain seven different reasons why she could not use the technique suggested. She was becoming more anxious with each new reason.

Then with great exasperation she blurted out, "But how can I be a good parent if I can't make him do what I want him to do, when I want him to do it? Just tell me how to make him come to the table, eat his dinner, and show a little appreciation for a nice meal by not arguing with us all the time!"

Sad but true, it may be impossible to find someone to tell her how to do that. She is asking for control over something she can never control. It is impossible to control the thoughts and actions of another person. The very best we can do, is to set up situations in which the other person decides it is best to do as asked. It makes us wonder which is most important, to control how our children act and think, or to give our kids 18 years worth of experiences that show them how the real world works. If we believe it is our job to control children, we will be inclined to operate like the mother in this story, who demanded that her child come to dinner *right now*.

If we believe our job is to help children discover how the real world operates and how to think for themselves, we will tend to act like the parent who says, "We will be serving dinner for the next 30 minutes. I sure hope you make it because we love eating with you."

❤

Great parents teach their children—rather than control them

97

"Just Say No" Isn't That Easy

IF YOUR SON HAD THE CHOICE OF EITHER dinner with the family, or a hamburger at the fast-food restaurant with his girlfriend, which would he choose? He'd probably go for the latter. That's because friends are very important to teens. Friends are a part of most teens' search for an identity of their own. A teen says to himself, "If I hang around with my parents all the time, do I know who I am? No!"

Wise parents understand the role friends play in their teen's social development. They say, "I know you need lots of time with your friends. I sure hope you can find a way to do this and still get your homework and chores done."

The Other Strong Voice

Problems arise when teens listen to their peers more than to themselves or their parents. Many think that listening to their parents proves they're not independent. The only other voice that's available belongs to their peers.

Some teens have actually been conditioned, by their parents, to listen to this other voice! This happens when we start telling our children, at an early age, to do things our way—or else.

When teens have been conditioned their entire lives to listen to another voice telling them what to do, they really aren't prepared to think for themselves! They simply replace their parent's voice with the voices of their peers.

Teach Your Kids to Think!

Children will listen to their own inner voice, if they have lots of chances to practice decision making. This begins early in life with

little choices like, "Would you like vanilla or chocolate ice cream?" or "Do you want to wear your red socks or blue socks?" The child then lives with the consequences of the decision. If the youngster is unhappy, the parent says, "Don't worry, you can choose again tomorrow." The decisions get bigger as a child gets older.

One thankful parent tells a story about his own son, Will, as an example of a teen who had important decisions to make. Will's two closest friends were an alcoholic and a drug user. Instead of trying to forbid the friendships, this parent said to Will, "With friends like yours, you get to make more decisions than anyone in school!"

He also said in a loving way, "They are lucky to have a friend like you. My guess is that some of you rubs off on them." Will confirmed this, saying his friends did not drink or take drugs around him.

It wasn't easy for this dad, who wondered if he was handling the situation in the best way. The worst thing parents can do is suggest peers will rub off on their own teens. That becomes a self-fulfilling prophecy.

It's normal for adolescents to listen to their peers. We can help them become independent, by allowing them to think and make decisions, beginning at a young age. Only then, will their own strong inner voice come across loud and clear.

❤

Help Your Child Develop a Strong Inner Voice

98

Taking Charge of Chronic Problems

The Strategic Training Session

YOUNG PEOPLE SEEM TO HAVE AN UNCANNY KNACK for knowing when their parents are vulnerable to "kid attack." They turn on their little radar sets and find ways to get the upper hand, just when we have the least amount of tactical support.

One dad said, "Little Erin behaves just great when we go somewhere she wants to go, but just let it be a grocery store trip for me and she goes wild. It always happens in public. Everybody stares, and I'm so embarrassed!"

This is something that happens to all of us. Once our children have played their hand a few times, waging war in public, we can counter with the Strategic Training Session.

The dad who told us about little Erin, recently employed the Strategic Training Session. He called his best friend saying, "I've been having trouble with Erin at the store and I need your help. Would you station yourself at the pay phone outside the mall tomorrow at 10:30?" They visited on the phone and set up the Strategic Training Session.

Dad and Erin shopped for groceries the next day, and Erin was her usual obnoxious self. Dad, in a quiet voice, asked, "Would you rather behave or go sit in your room?" Erin called Dad's bluff and continued to act out. The next thing Erin knew, she was being escorted to a phone in the store where Dad called his friend and said, "Shopping is not fun today. Please come!"

Erin, still figuring this to be a ploy, continued whining and begging. A minute later, her eyes grew large when she saw Dad's best friend walk up to her and say in a calm way, "Let's go to your room. You can wait for your father there."

Erin was sent to her room, while Dad had a quiet shopping trip and Dad's best friend watched TV. Erin was allowed to come out of her room as soon as Dad came home and she appeared happy to see him again. Dad was pleasant because he had had a great time all by himself.

Dad and his best friend set up another Strategic Training Session two days later. Erin started her usual store behavior with teary eyes and a whining mouth. However, when Dad asked if she would rather shape up or go to her room, her eyes opened wide and her mouth shut tight.

❤

ELEMENTS OF A STRATEGIC TRAINING SESSION
- Find someone who will help
- Schedule the session on a day when you have both the energy, and your support team available
- Play it cool; take good care of yourself
- Show no anger
- Schedule an additional practice session, within a short time, as a reinforcement

99

Getting Ready for School

"HOW MANY TIMES DO I HAVE TO CALL YOU? You get yourself moving! You're going to be late for school!" These are the desperate sounds of a frustrated parent trying to hurry a youngster through the morning ritual called "getting ready for school." Unfortunately, this child is moving at a snail's pace. This drama, played out in many homes every morning, starts the day off with a battle.

Children find creative ways to tell their parents how they feel. They seldom use words. Most often, they use actions to let us know they don't like the way things are being handled. Nothing is more confusing or frustrating to parents.

It would be much easier to be a parent if children would talk to us and say things such as, "I want to be able to think for myself. I'm dragging my feet so you can see that reminders won't work with me." However, they don't do this. Their way of getting us to understand, is to use actions such as slowing down when we push.

Parents aren't mind readers, so it's natural to misread their child's actions and assume that they are lazy or don't care. The natural reaction is to then push, punish, or remind them to change their behavior. The child then increases the actions to show that the parent is wrong, and the battle is on.

The first hour of the day is the very best time to teach children to be responsible, by allowing them to do most of their own thinking. It's also the time when parents can let their children do most of the work, since most jobs at that time of the day *really belong to the children.*

Use Consequences Instead of Threats and Anger

GUIDELINE 1:

Decide which jobs belong to the parent and which belong to the youngster— Jobs like setting the alarm the night before, waking up to the alarm, choosing clothes, dressing, washing, watching the clock, remembering lunch money and school supplies, and even deciding how much to eat really belong to the child. That doesn't leave much for the parent.

The only person who should suffer consequences if these jobs are neglected is the youngster. Let the school provide the consequences when the child is late.

GUIDELINE 2:

Stay out of the reminder business— Reminders rob children of the opportunity to make the mistakes needed to learn the lessons.

GUIDELINE 3:

Don't rescue!— Rescuing children robs them of the opportunity to learn lessons at emotional times when they will be best remembered. In other words, we don't put them in the car and take them to school, and we don't write an excuse to the teacher.

GUIDELINE 4:

Replace anger with sadness when children make mistakes— A wise parent, seeing their child is going to be late, says, "Oh, Honey, I'm sorry you're going to have a problem with your teacher. I sure hope you can work it out."

Loving parents have difficulty watching children learn from life's natural consequences. It's far easier to yell, threaten, and punish than it is to remain quiet and let children learn from experience. It's a strong parent who can allow a child to learn from his or her mistakes.

❤

*The first hour of the day is the very best time
to teach children to be responsible*

100

Don't Touch!

I HATE TO GO SHOPPING. I've hated it for as long as I can remember. A number of people in the past have tried to help me with my problem, but to no avail.

I had a flashback the other day. I was coping with yet another shopping excursion by watching parents deal with their kids, when I suddenly heard a slap followed by the sound of a screaming parent:

"How many times have I told you not to touch? Do you want to go into the rest room for another spanking? Don't you make me tell you one more time to keep your hands off the things! Don't touch! And I mean it!"

There was the flashback. I could see myself fifty years ago in Thrifty Drug Store in Los Angeles. There I was, going through the store, doing what little kids do, trying to be big by doing the same things the big people did.

The adults touched and examined the merchandise. I touched and examined the merchandise. Then I was reprimanded, and my hands were slapped.

Human beings, by nature, are copying animals. This means we learn best by watching others and imitating their behavior. That is one of the reasons we have so many habits, values, and mannerisms that are similar to those of our own parents.

This imitating happens on the subconscious level. We are never actually aware of it taking place. Psychologists call it learning through modeling.

Many of the battles I see in the shopping centers between kids and parents can be traced back to this issue of modeling. Unfortunately, many parents are frustrated when their kids try to act like adults.

There Is a Solution

STEP ONE:

Teach your children to act in independent, yet responsible, ways. For instance, many parents have found it helpful to spend a little time teaching their children how to be responsible shoppers. They teach their children how to touch the merchandise, when to touch, and when not to touch.

STEP TWO:

Let your youngster know you only touch things you can afford to pay for in case of an accident. This gives you something to say instead of, "Don't touch." From this point on, it will be more effective to ask, "That costs twenty-nine dollars. Can you afford to pay for it?" Most children will say, "But I won't break it." The adult's answer at this point should be, "That's not the point. We agreed that you can touch things you can afford to buy. Please put it back."

STEP THREE:

Some time is spent actually practicing in a store on items that are unbreakable. Tell your youngster the two of you are going into the store today to look at things and practice deciding which things should and should not be touched. Then spend a little time practicing the right way to touch, and how to put things back.

STEP FOUR:

Now it is time to catch the child doing it right so you can provide some positive reinforcement. "Look how well you are doing. It makes me happy to see you acting so grown up." In the event things are not going well, you can ask, "What was our agreement about that?"

STEP FIVE:

Once the lesson is taught, and there have been opportunities for practice, you can provide a short little review before you walk into a shopping area: "Tell me how you plan to handle your shopping. I'm anxious to hear how well you can do."

❤

Teach your children to act in independent yet responsible ways

Chapter
Eleven

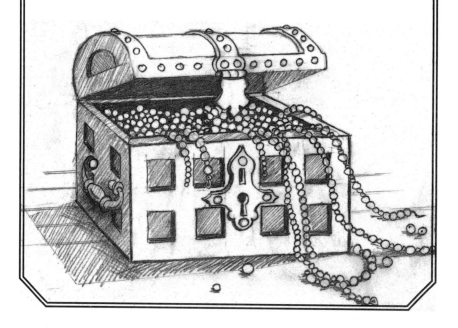

101

TV and "Mush-Brain"

EVERY NEW MEDIA STUDY seems to bring on increased parental anxiety. The headlines are alarming: "Average child watches five hours of TV a day." "Experts claim television is the dominant influence on American kids."

We read the reports, cast a wary eye toward the family room, where our kids are imitating potted plants in front of the tube, and we shake our heads in dismay. "Those kids," we say, "watch too much TV. They are going to suffer from 'Mush Brain.'"

We are forever devising strategies to curtail our kids' TV habits. With television watching, as with many other issues, our modeling is the key. It's pretty hard for a major league couch potato to come down hard on his or her child's TV habits.

To influence our kids' TV habits, we must emphasize the alternatives—playing up the good things about friends, family, hobbies, sports, and so on. Consider the following discussion between a dad and his TV-watching son.

DAD: "I've noticed you're watching a lot of TV lately. You like it, don't you?"
BILL: "Yeah. I like it a lot."
DAD: "The good thing about TV is that you can learn a lot. You can find out what's happening in the world. It helps your vocabulary, and you can learn about grown-ups. But one thing I'm wondering about is how much you think you learn about being a good friend. Are you a good friend to your TV set?"
BILL: "I don't know what you mean."
DAD: "The TV doesn't listen much to you, does it? It just talks at

you. It doesn't care about what you say, right?"

BILL: "Uh . . . right."

DAD: "So, one thing about a TV set is it doesn't help you be a good friend to anyone. Does it ever pay attention to what you say? Does it ever listen to you?"

BILL: "No."

DAD: "What I think about TV is, it doesn't give a darn about you. That's the problem with the TV. However, your friends and I listen to you. But the TV doesn't really care what you think. I think if you watch a lot of TV, you can be really smart about many things. But I don't know if you'll ever be able to prove it because you don't learn how to talk by watching TV. You might be happier, in the long run, if you watch less. But whose decision is it?"

BILL: "Mine."

DAD: "Yes, it really is. Hey, let me feel your brain. It doesn't feel too soft. I guess 'Mush Brain' hasn't set in—yet!"

It's best not to set ourselves up for a control battle over TV watching with commands and threats. Harping at our kids constantly, or imposing severe cuts in their viewing habits, often leads to rebellion.

What we can do, however, is influence our kids. A generous dose of humor does wonders. It is also helpful to remember that very few youngsters would rather watch TV than do something fun with their parents. Many experts advise us to either watch TV with our children so we can have some control, interpret for children what they see, or invite our children to do something with us instead.

❤

Few youngsters would rather watch TV than do something fun with their parents

102

When to Seek Professional Help

A DELICATE QUESTION OFTEN ARISES from parents of troublesome children: "When should we decide to seek professional help?"

Seeking professional help is not an admission of failure. In our complex society, with it's myriad social problems, our teens quite naturally face dilemmas that we never had to cope with during our childhood. Societal pressures for success, for example, are overwhelming, filtering down even to the lower grades. Peer pressure prompts children to insist on Calvin Klein jeans and Air Jordan sneakers—when they're still in kindergarten! More children have severe problems than ever before, and the causes of those problems stand apart from the method, or intent, of parental discipline.

There are two basic guidelines to follow for seeking professional help

1. If a situation has gotten progressively worse over a three-month period, with no improvement in sight, professional help may be necessary.

2. If your teen, who's been basically good, responsible, and responsive, suddenly changes his/her total demeanor (grades go down dramatically, friendships drop off) you may want to seek professional help immediately.

Be advised that professional care does not necessarily mean a long drawn-out series of counseling sessions. Oftentimes, one session, with a trained counselor who knows what he or she is talking about, is enough to straighten out the problem.

Guidelines for finding the right professional care:

1. Find a therapist who has a busy schedule. Someone who is busy with many clients, must be on the right track.

2. Seek out satisfied clients. Ask the therapist to give you a list of a few satisfied clients you can talk with.

3. A good therapist should be willing to give you a free half-hour session to discuss your situation.

4. Look at what's going on with the professional. Does he/she have a good marriage? Are his/her children well adjusted?

5. Get recommendations. Talk with pediatricians, school counselors, and psychiatric or pediatric nurses. Pick the person whose name comes up three times. If hospitalization is recommended, make sure the person recommending it is working outside the hospital system.

❤

Seeking professional help is not an admission of failure

103

"Don't Roll Your Eyes at Me!"

"EVERY TIME I ASK SONDRA TO DO SOMETHING, or even when I want to talk to her, it happens," one mom said. "She slumps her shoulders and kind of tilts her head a little, and then she gives me this look that could open oysters at fifty paces. It really fries me. I don't know what to do about it."

Negative body language. Those irritating shows of displeasure our children throw at us when we ask them to do something they don't want to do, or talk about something they don't want to talk about.

Most parents read these messages to mean their children are copping a bad attitude. What does Sondra really mean when she fires that icy glare at her mom? Is she disappointed, angry at herself, trying to say that Mom's unfair, saying that she feels hurt, let down, or criticized, or what? Sondra's mom doesn't know for sure, but it is natural for her to assume that it is directed at her. This assumption often leads to unnecessary trouble.

The best response is to say what we have to say, and then walk away. Negative body language is not a problem for us if we don't see it, and if we don't make a problem out of it. However, if it continues, we need to think about our own behavior. What did we do or say the instant before our child shot his or her eyes toward the sky? Did we criticize? Is he or she merely reacting to that criticism?

Kids are like adults when it comes to taking criticism, they react to it, often in a negative way. The time to deal with this negative behavior is when both parent and child are calm and reasonably happy. It's a good time to get to the root of the problem:

MOM: "Hey, Sondra, is this a good time to talk?"

SONDRA: "Yeah, I guess so."

MOM: "You know, I've been noticing when I say something to you, you give me your nuclear fission look, and I have a hard time reading what that really means. Some kids do that because they don't feel it's safe to say they're hurt or disappointed. Some kids do that because they're unhappy. Other kids do it because they hate their parent and wish they would shut up. Do you have any thoughts on that?"

SONDRA: "No."

MOM: "I would sure like to hear about it if you do. One thing I'm thinking is, maybe I'm doing something to put you down or criticize you. If you feel you're up to telling me something about that, I'd sure like to be a good listener."

Then Mom should drop the issue and see what happens.

If the negative body language is such a constant that we can successfully predict when it will happen, we might preface our remarks to our child with a comment like, "Hey, Sondra, I have something I want to share with you. Now, when I get through, you might want to try to melt me with that laser look you're so good at, so you might want to get it ready just in case." This will be a double bind for Sondra, and probably will eliminate the laser look, at least this time.

❤

Negative Body Language Is Best Dealt with at Happy Times

104

Good Parents Don't Give Warnings

THINK OF YOURSELF TOOLING DOWN THE FREEWAY at 70 mph in a 55 mph zone. You see the multicolored lights in your rearview mirror, and you think of one thing, and one thing only: "I'm going to get a ticket."

The cop saunters up to your car, nice as can be, writes the ticket, bids you adieu, and is on his merry way. He offers no hysterics, no anger, no threats; just courtesy, and a little slip of paper—the consequences of your breaking the law.

As an adult, you would never think of telling him, "I'll be good, officer. Honest, I won't speed anymore," and having him say, "Well, okay. If you'll be good, I won't write you a ticket." That is the stuff of fantasy. How often do we allow the fantasy world to become reality for our children?

Jerry comes home late.

Mom, thinking she's consequential, says, "We'll talk about this in the morning. Off to your room."

Jerry says, "I'm sorry I'm late. Time just got away from us. I promise it won't happen again."

What does Mom say but, "Oh well, okay. Are you sure you'll be in before curfew next time you go out? Or are you going to keep me worrying until all hours of the morning? I've told you before what's going to happen if you don't remember to get in on time."

"I know, Mom. I won't do it anymore."

"Well, okay," Mom says, thinking her problems are over. "Go to bed."

The real world doesn't operate on the multiple warning system, and neither should parents. Parents who give a lot of warnings, raise children who don't behave until they've had a lot of warnings.

The real world operates on consequences. If we do a lousy job at work, our boss doesn't take away our VCR. He fires us. By allowing teens to feel the results of naturally occurring consequences, parents then allow teens to learn about their responsibilities and their behavior. Consequences lead to self-examination and thought.

Mom, after seeing Jerry come home late, can handle the situation in the following way, allowing consequences to fall.

After Jerry comes in, Mom says, "I really worried about you. I'm glad you're home. Go on to bed and we'll talk about this when we're calm."

Then Mom doesn't say anything more about it, until the next time Jerry wants to go out and Mom drops the bomb: "Oh, Honey, I think you ought to stay home. I'm not up to worrying about you tonight."

The consequences fall like a bolt out of the blue.

❤

The Real World Doesn't Operate on the Multiple Warning System

105

"I'm Bored" Routine

IT'S THREE HOURS AFTER THE DAWN OF CHRISTMAS MORNING, and calm has replaced flying paper and frantic squeals of delight. Toys, toys, and more toys litter the floor—enough diversion to keep three day-care centers going for years. Then, from the rubble, a sad little face emerges and a doleful voice is heard. "Mommy, I'm bored."

Our inevitable response is, "What? Bored? You've got more toys than all the kids in the Third World put together, and you're bored? No, it's a psychological impossibility."

Bored children put dread in the first day of summer vacation. Continual cries of, "Daddy, what can I do?" make us long for the day when the big yellow buses resume their daily rounds.

Despite what our children say, they probably aren't bored. When children say they are bored, it usually means, "I want you to spend more time with me."

Playing with our children is one of the great joys of parenting. When we agree to do so, we should make it plain to them that their boredom is their problem. The parent in the following discussion handled the problem well:

CHILD: I'm bored. There's nothing going on around here."
PARENT: "Are you really bored? That's too bad. What are your plans?"
CHILD: "Well, what can I do?"
PARENT: "That's a really good question. What kind of things are in your room?"
CHILD: "Aw, there's nothing in there that I like. I'm tired of it all."
PARENT: "Well, are there things that you like anywhere else in the house?"

CHILD: "I don't think so."

PARENT: "A lot of people get involved with things that they like so they won't be bored. You're saying when you're bored, there's nothing you really like?"

CHILD: "Right."

PARENT: "So, it looks to me like there may not be any other option than to sit and be bored. Would you say that was a possibility?"

CHILD: "I guess I could play with my video game."

PARENT: "Would you like me to play one game with you?"

CHILD: "Yeah!"

PARENT: "I guess I could play one game. But if I do that, do you think you'll say, 'Oh thank you,' or will you whine and say, 'Oh, please, play one more?' How will you handle it if I play one game with you?"

CHILD: "I promise not to ask for another game."

We want our children to develop the ability to motivate, interest, and entertain themselves. Allow them to poke their way out of their self-imposed shell of boredom, rather than providing them with an entertainment service.

❤

"I'm bored" usually means,
"I want to spend more time with you"

106

Teenage Transportation

TEENAGE TRANSPORTATION IS A THOUGHT-PROVOKING ISSUE for parents. Transportation issues include other children carting our child around, our carting our own child around, and sometimes, and most worrisome, our child carting his or her own self around.

Before teens learn to drive, parents must explore, with them, the new dangers they're going to be facing. Some parents handle the transportation issue by laying down the law. Other parents handle it by getting their teens to think about life in the fast lane. Effective parents hold a conversation similar to:

DAD: "Katie, if you were to die before you were 21, and I hope you don't, how, statistically, would you die?"
KATIE: "I don't know."
DAD: "Oh, I bet you do. What are the two major ways teens die?"
KATIE: "Suicide?"
DAD: "Right. Do you think you're the suicidal type?"
KATIE: "No . . ."
DAD: "I don't either. So you probably won't die by suicide. How would you die?"
KATIE: "Car accident?"
DAD: "Right! If you were to die before you were 21, it would probably be in a car accident. And generally, in these car accidents, there is something else involved. What's that?"
KATIE: "Alcohol."
DAD: "You're right. Do you think about this much, or don't you think about it much?"
KATIE: "I don't think about it much."

DAD: "That's what I thought. Now, considering the kids that die, do you think they think about it a lot, or do you think they probably don't?"
KATIE: "I suppose they don't."
DAD: "Right. So you fit the profile. Anyway, I just want you to know that I love you and would miss you if you were killed before you are 21."
KATIE: "I know, Dad. I'll be careful."
DAD: "Thanks."

There are other general rules for teenage transportation. First, wise parents consider offering their teen "good guy" auto insurance. "Good guy" auto insurance means the parents pay the premium based on the child having a "B" average in school, a flawless driving record, and in most states, having completed driver's education. Then, if the child does have a ticket, or if his or her grades are poor, the parent can respond with sorrow, not anger, and say, "Gee, what a bummer for you. Your insurance is going to go up now. How do you think you'll pay for the increase?"

Finally, a word of caution. In most states, children may get their driver's licenses when they are chronologically sixteen. However, many children who are chronologically sixteen are socially and emotionally age fourteen or younger. Such children may have repeated several grades and, at sixteen, are in junior high school. It is a wise parent who discourages their teen from receiving a license until he or she is socially or emotionally sixteen years of age. Generally speaking, that means the teen is functioning on an eleventh grade level.

❤

Discuss transportation issues with your teen by getting him/her to think about life in the fast lane

107

Social and Extracurricular Activities

PARENTS AND TEENS OFTEN FIND THEMSELVES in the heat of battle over extracurricular activities. These battles are usually centered around the parents' belief that the activities are not acceptable. As parents, we often confuse acceptance with approval. There is a big difference. For instance, we can accept the fact there are wars. It doesn't mean that we have to approve of them. This means we can listen to a discussion about war without being afraid that we are giving the impression we approve of war.

As parents, we hope our teens will discuss many of the things that go on in their lives. Like adults, teens make mistakes or find themselves in difficult situations. It is helpful for them to be able to talk with an interested, not blaming, adult about these experiences. The fact that they are willing to talk to us is a good sign. It gives them a chance to relive, in a safe way, what happened, and get their own beliefs in order. Effective parents listen without being afraid that their willingness to listen, in a nonblaming way, means approval.

A parent who is able to listen with interest, curiosity, and sincere questions about the teen's thoughts, opinions, or values, can actually help the youngster look at these situations in a healthy way. Parents who use this approach, find the more they listen, the more their teens actually start evaluating the wisdom of the activity.

Parents who are quick to be critical, or to restrict and punish, soon teach their teens to withhold information. At the same time, they greatly reduce the amount of thought the youngster gives to an

activity. Teens who have critical parents, spend more time defending their actions and thoughts than they do thinking about the activity.

Wise parents are more concerned about their teen's plans for handling undesirable activities than they are about restricting those activities. Whether an activity is good or bad is not nearly as important as knowing your teen can handle any temptations associated with the extracurricular activity. The following scenario illustrates this:

TEEN: "Mom, I'm old enough to go to that concert. Can I go?"

MOM: "I'll know you're old enough when you can tell me about the possible pressures you're going to have to face, and your plan for handling them."

TEEN: "Geez, Mom. Are you worried I'll do drugs? You know I don't do drugs."

MOM: "That's not what I said. I want to know what you are going to say when the other kids are telling you that everybody does drugs at a concert and that you're not going to get hooked if you do some once in a while."

TEEN: "Geez, Mom. Don't you trust me?"

MOM: "That's not the point. I know how hard it is to be in awkward situations. I also know that once you have thought it out, and come up with a plan for handling those situations, you'll be ready to take care of yourself. I'll be glad to let you go to the concert when you can describe that plan to me."

This mother knows that the day this teen can describe her plan for handling an activity is the day that she is ready for the activity and that Mom no longer needs to worry.

❤

Acceptance of extracurricular activities is not the same as approval. Wise parents accept the activity, and help their teen learn to handle the temptations that may be associated with that activity.

108

If We Could Only Raise Kids Instead of Mirrors

FOR YEARS, WELL-KNOWN EDUCATIONAL CONSULTANT Jim Fay, has suggested parents avoid telling children how to solve their problems. Instead, ask if the youngster would like to hear what other children have tried. Offer a menu of possible solutions, ranging from the worst possible solution to the best.

Then ask the youngster to look at the possible consequences of each choice, before deciding on a course of action. This is a win-win situation. The child either makes a good choice and feels good about it, or makes a bad one and gains wisdom through the experience of a poor choice.

These kinds of techniques usually make so much sense to parents, they rush home to try them on the children. Susan Anderson was no exception. It's obvious from the following dialogue that she not only learned the new strategy, but used it well.

In fact, she was such a good model for her child, that she found herself writing to Jim with one of those "what now" questions.

Susan wrote that after she had tried her new information, her five-year-old came to her and said, "Gee, Mom, it looks like you've got a problem."

"Oh," said Mom.

"Your kids need more toys! They need more Cherry Merry Muffin Kitchen stuff."

"Oh," replied Mom.

"Would you like to know how other parents have handled this?"

"I guess so," said Mom.

"Some have bought more toys. Others just give the money to the kids. Let me know what you decide."

Then the child fell on the floor laughing.

The letter ended with, "Jim—now what?"

The best advice would be to smile and say, "Nice try! You did that so well. I just know you're going to be a great mommy someday." Give the youngster a big hug and have some fun with the fact that she is learning by imitating.

Unfortunately, we find that our children become mirrors for us. They imitate our actions, our tone of voice, our attitudes, our values, and even our fears. Copying is the way humans learn best. Regardless of how we lead our lives, we raise children who are no more than mirrors of our own behavior.

❤

Our Children Become Mirrors—They Imitate Our Actions,
Our Tone of Voice, Our Attitudes, Our Values, and Even Our Fears

109

Consistent Messages Produce Positive Results

WHEN PARENTS GIVE INCONSISTENT MESSAGES, they tend to raise negativistic and strong-willed children. As most children learn from modeling, the parent may not be modeling behavior they want the child to grow into! In short, it is hard for a child to really respect an inconsistent parent.

Two Guidelines to Follow in Order to Be Consistent

Too many rules can cause parents to be inconsistent, or paint themselves into a corner. For example, you may decide your teen cannot stay out past 11:00 p.m., and then a special occasion comes along and you allow him/her to stay out later than 11:00 p.m. You have become inconsistent in your message. Instead of making hard-and-fast rules, treat each situation on an individual basis.

Sometimes parents are inconsistent because they give a consequence without really thinking it through. Parents are usually inconsistent if they come up with a consequence when they are angry.

An example might be, "Cindy, you're grounded for two weeks!" Later Cindy comes and says, "Gee, Dad, next week is the Senior Prom. Surely, you're not going to be so cruel and ground me from that?" The father is in a bind. If he doesn't go back on his word, and is consistent, he's really mean. On the other hand, giving in may breed disrespect. It's better to wait for calm times to consequence your teen's behavior.

Teens Have Three Options

Teens who hear inconsistent messages tend to think:

- Their parent doesn't think things through, but rather shoots from the hip
- Wonders if their parent is basically a pushover
- Wonders if their parent has their best interests at heart

Parents can change:

Parents who give inconsistent messages can change by first admitting they are inconsistent, and allowing the other parent to handle certain situations.

Or the inconsistent parent can talk it over with his/her teen:

"You know, John, I don't think I'm helping you very much because I'm inconsistent. I tell you one thing one minute, and then I tell you another thing another minute. I bet that leads you to think I don't know what I'm talking about most of the time. So I'm going to try and do less of that. If you see me being inconsistent, you may want to remind me about it in a thoughtful way."

Keep in mind, though, your teen may only remind you when it's in his/her favor to do so.

Consistent Parents . . .

1. Treat each situation on an individual basis, instead of making hard-and-fast rules.
2. Wait for calm times to consequence behavior.

110

The Shy Child

THERE ARE THREE MAJOR REASONS THAT CHILDREN appear shy and withdrawn. First, many children are simply built that way. They are good and responsive children who simply have never liked the attention of strangers. Such children may be shy because of their genetic makeup. Badgering can only make this situation worse.

Children may be shy because they have suffered from strangers or families. They have learned not to trust others.

Finally, children may be shy and retiring because this is a "hook" that they unconsciously use to upset their parents. Children want emotion from their parents. They'll do almost anything to get it. If a child learns that being shy and withdrawn gets the parent's goat and leads to parental frustration, the child will naturally become even more shy and withdrawn as time passes.

No matter what the cause, parents best handle the situation by accepting the child for who he or she is. The parent might say something like:

"Well, Jane, the thing I like about you is that you think things over before you say anything. More than that, you are careful about who you make friends with. You don't just rush in there like some children and make friends willingly. You like to think about it. Of course, sometimes, you think about it so hard that you may have fewer friends. But, then again, Jane, everybody is different!"

Some children do give the appearance of being pathologically shy and withdrawn. They simply won't talk to anybody about anything. In this situation, professional help may be needed. A thoughtful and wise therapist may be able to form a trusting relationship with a child in

play therapy, and help the child express him or herself verbally and have, consequently, less need to withdraw. If a child is shy and withdrawn secondary to trauma, professional help may be necessary.

Finally, it may be helpful to *encourage*, but not *badger*, shy children. Parents might say, "Boy, I bet John would really be happy if you talked to him. I'll bet that boy would like to have your friendship! I think maybe you'll decide that you'll want to talk to him."

Such conversation has a much better chance of succeeding than saying, "Why don't you talk to John? You're just too shy."

❤

It's Helpful to Encourage Shy Children, Not Badger Them

Chapter Twelve

111

Teens and Television

PARENTS OFTEN BELIEVE THEY HELP THEIR TEENAGERS by controlling *what* they watch on television. Good parenting, they believe, is monitoring the massive amounts of television trash their teens may pour into their heads. However, it may be more appropriate for parents to set limits on *quantity*, rather than *quality*.

In analyzing his practice over the past 20 years, adult and child psychiatrist Foster W. Cline, M.D., says he has come to the conclusion that it's *not what* teens watch, but that they even *watch* television. Dr. Cline says he has never seen a child hurt or helped from the content of television. He explains he has never run into a person who grew up in a dysfunctional family who felt his/her life had been improved by watching television. For instance, Dr. Cline says he hasn't had a patient state, "Well, actually, Dr. Cline, I grew up in an unhappy and strange family, but I watched a lot of Beaver Cleaver and Cosby shows, and so I didn't turn out so bad." Likewise, he's never seen a normal child growing up in a loving and healthy family whose personality or behavior was made significantly worse by watching shows of violence.

No, it's not what they watch that is affecting America's youth. It's that they watch so much. Not everything about television is negative. Television encourages the passive reception of concepts— which, to a point, is good. However, many teens watch hundreds of hours of television. They watch more hours than they spend in school. They watch more hours than they spend with their parents! Sometimes, they spend more hours with the television than they spend doing anything active with friends.

Teachers across the nation report, teenagers respond in the classroom as if they were watching television. Teens sit and look intelligent. They soak up the knowledge. They absorb. They just don't do much—no classroom participation, no homework, nothing!

The greatest sorrow, however, is that responsibility for this situation doesn't rest primarily with teens. It rests with the parents. Early on, television and videos can become very convenient baby-sitters. When a young child gets fussy, it's often easier to pop in a Disney video than to help the child occupy him- or herself. A child who has not learned to occupy his or her time with creative activities, may become a teen who chooses television over friends, family, or activities.

It's time for parents to have fun with their teens again and encourage them to get involved in activities away from the television. Instead of monitoring what teens watch, parents must monitor how much they watch.

❤

It's more appropriate for parents to set limits on quantity rather than quality

112

Turning Bad Decisions into Wisdom

THERE ARE MANY DIFFERENT WAYS TO CAUSE CHILDREN to carry the lion's share of the thinking. There are many different ways to force decision making, and there are many unique and creative ways to express genuine sadness for children who make mistakes.

A father recently reminded me of the beauty of considering childhood mistakes as opportunities to gain wisdom and experience. He related the following opportunity his 12-year-old provided for himself.

Dad received a call from the police station notifying him his son had been picked up for shoplifting. A million things ran through his mind as he drove to pick up his son.

He thought about ranting, raving, and rescuing. He also thought about using empathy instead, to drive the pain of this lesson home. He remembered that a consequence needs to become the bad guy, while the parent becomes the good guy.

Dad met a very sheepish child at the detention center. "Don't be mad, Dad. I'm sorry. I'll never do anything this stupid again!"

"I'm not mad, son, but I really feel sorry for what you're going to have to go through. I guess you know you'll have to appear in court. Who knows what the judge will do. I'd suggest you call around to some law offices and find out how much you're going to have to pay to be represented in court."

The boy got his courage up and made some calls. Later he came to his dad in a state of depression. "Dad, do you know that the cheapest lawyer I could find wants to charge me $600? That's a rip-off!"

"It's always expensive to hire professional help. Maybe I can help you. In this state parents can represent their children in court.

If you want, I'll do it for half price. But maybe you want to think about that for a while. Let me know what you decide."

The child thought for a moment and said, "I guess I better have you represent me. But I don't even have $300. If you do it, will you loan me the money?"

Dad said he'd loan him the money. However, the boy was in for some more big surprises. This father took his son to the office supply store and purchased a legal promissory note form. The two of them sat down together, filled out the form, and the son signed the document.

Father and son finally appeared before the judge of the juvenile court. "Young man, are you represented by counsel?" asked the judge.

"Yes sir. My Dad's not a lawyer, but he agreed to do it for me for half price. He even loaned me the money and made me put up collateral and sign a promissory note."

"How do you plead in this matter?" asked the judge.

Dad said, "My client is pleading guilty, Your Honor."

"Fine," answered the judge. "Do you have anything to say before I rule?"

"Yes, Your Honor," offered Dad. "This is a good boy. He's never been in trouble before. He admits that he made a big mistake and does not plan to repeat this behavior. He is requesting that you consider a deferred judgment. He is even suggesting that the period of time be 12 months instead of the regular six-month deferred judgment so he can prove to the court he can stay out of trouble for that period of time."

The judge struck his gavel and said, "So ordered. Stay out of trouble, young man. Now stand down!"

Father and son left the courtroom together, walking to their car. As they settled into their seats for the trip home, the boy looked over at his dad and said, "You know what, Dad? You were awesome in there!"

I think we would all agree, this was a time when something that could have become a tragedy, was turned into a great learning opportunity. I bet we would also all agree, this young boy has a lot more respect and love for his dad.

❤

Express genuine sadness when your child makes a mistake

113

Avoiding Control Battles

AVOIDING CONTROL BATTLES IS NOT ALWAYS EASY, but is an essential, learnable skill. Such battles often occur when a parent gives their teen an order the parent can't enforce, such as: "Pick up that stuff right now." "Move fast." "You're not leaving this house with *that* on." Teens will find many other things to do, rather than pick up their stuff, "right now." No one can *make* a teen move faster. Many teens sigh and move more slowly when asked to speed up.

In most situations, where parents give orders, they should start their sentences with the word "if." "If" can always be used to indicate choices and consequences. For instance, the parent might say, "If you get your stuff picked up by dinner, then you'll be eating with us," or, "If you move really fast, I'll feel like moving fast for you, and I'll start dinner."

Using enforceable statements is another essential element in avoiding control battles. When using these, the wise parent talks about himself or herself: "I will be doing the laundry that has been brought down to the laundry room," or "I will fix dinner, as soon as the rooms are clean."

Unwise parents set up control battles by saying things like, "We're leaving at 8:00, you've got to be ready." Even United Airlines doesn't say, "We're leaving at 8:00, you've got to be ready!" United says, "We're leaving at 8:00, and if you're there 10 minutes ahead of departure, we won't give your seat away."

Control battles can be avoided by parents and teens problem solving together:

PARENT: "Honey, do you have a minute?"

TEEN: "Yeah, sure."

PARENT: "Lately you've been leaving your schoolwork scattered throughout the house."

TEEN: "Yeah, I know."

PARENT: "What's a solution? What do you want to do about it?"

TEEN: "Put it all away, I guess."

PARENT: "Well, that would be great! That would handle it this time. But this seems to be happening a lot. What do you want to do about it all the time?"

TEEN: "Put it away after I leave it out."

PARENT: "That would be great. What if you still forget? It's easy to forget, you know."

TEEN: "You pick it up?"

PARENT: "Well, maybe I could. How about if I just sweep through the place and put all your stuff in a garbage bag and put it in the rec room? Then you'd know where it is and it would only take me a second."

TEEN: "All my books and shoes and stuff together?"

PARENT: "Yeah, probably."

TEEN: "I think I'll remember to pick it all up."

PARENT: "Well, I hope so, but I do understand that forgetting is easy."

This parent avoided a control battle by problem solving around consequences, without anger. It's simple once parents practice and get the knack.

❤

RULES FOR AVOIDING CONTROL BATTLES:

1. Don't give an order that you cannot enforce.

2. Tell the teen how you stand, rather than what he or she must do.

3. Give the teen choices.

4. Problem solve together, while understanding your teen's feelings.

5. Give only reasonable consequences that you can live with yourself.

6. If you've made a mistake with your teen,
admit it without overdoing the apology.

7. Parent's expression of frustration and anger almost always means there has been a control battle, and worse yet, the teen has won!

114

The One-Year Plan

A Parent's Guide to Helping Children Succeed in School

1. Remember that parents can't teach for teachers, and teachers can't parent for parents. Remember that teachers can't learn for kids, and kids can't teach for teachers.

2. Show the same amount of love for your children, regardless of their success in school. Show sadness, rather than anger, when they have trouble at school.

3. Expect your children to do their share of chores at home.

4. Spend some time each day talking with excitement about your work and your day. Your children will want to imitate you and will soon begin to talk about school and their day.

5. Take turns reading to each other every day.

6. Have your children teach you something they have learned at school. Do this once per week.

7. Encourage your children to do things that "recharge their batteries." Encourage them to try many different activities as a way of discovering interests and talents. Remind them that they will build their careers around their talents, not around their weaknesses.

8. Provide a time and place for homework. Expect that your children will study. Allow them to either study by writing the assignments or thinking hard about them for a reasonable amount of time. If they decide to study by thinking, instead of writing or reading, have them think of a plan for explaining it to the teacher.

- Support the teacher.
- Don't fight with children over homework.
- Don't fight with the teachers over grades or the consequence for poor grades.
- Tell your children you will love them regardless of their grades, or the number of years it takes them to complete each grade.

9. Don't pay your children for good grades and don't punish for bad grades. Be excited about the good grades and sad for your children about their bad grades.

10. Have your children bring home school papers.
- Look at the right answers instead of the wrong ones.
- Don't correct the wrong answers—leave this for the teacher.
- Have your children explain the reasons for the right answers.
- If they don't know, give them three choices:
    1. You cheated?
    2. You tried hard?
    3. You are getting smarter in that subject?

11. Expect this program to take about one year before you see good results.
- Remember, children who have a hard time at school, need to get away from it for a while each day. More homework, and problems at home about school, won't help.
- Don't complain to teachers that they should give this child more homework. Use this program instead, and you will see amazing results in one year. Fight with your children and their teachers about homework, and the problem will still be there in years to come.

❤

Show the same amount of love for your child regardless of their success in school

115

The Masks of Poor Self-Image

PEOPLE WHO HAVE A STRONG SELF-IMAGE feel good about who they are. They have the ability to cope well in school, at home, or on the job. They know how to get along with their coworkers, friends, or family. They have a jump-start on life.

Unfortunately, some youngsters grow up without the benefit of strong self-esteem, often because their parents have concentrated more on their weaknesses than on their strengths. As teens, they may lack motivation, get poor grades, argue with their parents and teachers, bully their friends, act irresponsibly, or withdraw from social situations. These are some of the masks worn by a teen who suffers from a poor self-image.

The good news is that it is not too late to help these adolescents. Self-concept can be nurtured at any age.

Self-image is like a computer— Rooted in the subconscious mind, an individual's self-image is the result of everything he or she has experienced during a lifetime. As in a computer, the information stored in the subconscious is constantly growing and changing. Like a computer, the subconscious mind cannot tell the difference between right or wrong, real or imagined. Instead, everything is considered fact. In simplest terms, a person's self-image is the sum total of all the positive and negative messages he or she has experienced. Building self-image, then, becomes a matter of shifting the balance of messages and experiences to the positive end of the scale.

Self-image builders— Ways that parents unknowingly contribute to their teenager's lack of self-esteem include acting too suspicious,

setting up too many rules, or being overly critical. In place of this, parents are encouraged to help their teen build self-esteem in the following ways:

1. Help Teens Build on Their Strengths

An activity or skill that allows an individual to excel does wonders for their self-esteem. Parents need to help their teens identify what interests them and how they can get involved, regardless of whether it's debate, drama, chess, sports, or music.

Wise parents show excitement and enthusiasm about their teen's interests, even if we secretly wish they were involved in some other activity. An important rule to remember is that parents should never tear down, or take away, something that their teen does well.

2. Give Fewer Rules

Parents often forget that teens are at an age when they need fewer, not more, rules. When we take away too much freedom, we send the message that they are incapable of making good decisions for themselves. This tends to rob teens of growing experiences that teach them they are capable.

3. Emphasize the Positive

Parents should remember to give their teens more positive than negative messages. Teens are usually highly sensitive to criticism about their looks, clothes, or interests. Criticism tears down a fragile self-image even further.

❤

Build on strengths, give fewer rules, and emphasize the positive

116

"No" Is Not a Four-Letter Word

YOUNG PEOPLE NEED TO KNOW THEIR PARENTS are able to say "no" and mean it. However, our children rarely thank us for having the strength to set limits. Instead, they may pout, stomp around, run to their rooms, whine, or talk back. This often leaves the adult angry and confused.

Why are children so testy when we do what's best for them? Children who have no external controls, often misbehave as a way of getting us to provide enough control for them to feel confident about their place in the world. Children need to test limits to make sure they are firm. Some children use anger, some use guilt, some are sneaky, while others prefer to test our resolve when we say "no."

It helps to remember young people hear the word "no" far too often. "No" is a fighting word. Youngsters may wage war against "no" in subtle ways. They may try to get their parents to do all the thinking, while they stand back in judgment. Their opening ploy is often, "Why?" or "Why can't I?" or "Why do I have to?"

Parents who are busy reasoning with their children have neither the time, nor energy, to win battles. Caring parents who feel guilty about saying "no," so often are soon hooked into doing lots of thinking and explaining. All the youngster has to do now is interrupt the parent's explanations from time to time with, "But Dad, it's just not fair. You just don't understand." Soon the parent is worn down and gives in. "All right! Take it! But this is the last time."

You can turn the tables on children, forcing them to do most of the thinking. State your decision without saying "no." Then, whatever the youngster says, simply agree *that* is probably true *and* repeat your original decision. This is called Negative Assertion.

Here's how it can work in practice:

TEEN: "I need some money to go to the movies."

DAD: "Feel free to use your allowance."

TEEN: "I need more money."

DAD: "That's sad. But there will be more coming on Saturday."

TEEN: "I promised the guys."

DAD: "I'm sure that's true...and...you'll be getting more money on Saturday."

TEEN: "But I won't have enough money for gas for the car."

DAD: "I'm sure that's true, too...and...there will be more on Saturday."

TEEN: "Gee! Money is such a big deal to you."

DAD: "That could be true, too...and...."

TEEN: "I know, I know, you don't have to say it again."

❤

State your decisions without saying "no"

117

"That's Not the Way I Do It!"

"THAT'S NOT THE WAY I DO IT!" Those could be the words of either parents frustrated by their teen's growing need for independence or a teen trying to establish his or her own identity. Either way, the words represent an all too common battle of wills.

Most parents want the best for their children. We pray they will go through life always making wise decisions about issues like drugs, alcohol, school, careers, and friends. We recognize they are growing up in a complicated era in which the price of bad decisions can be high, and even dangerous.

Our teens are at an age when they no longer automatically buy into our values. They are seeking their own individuality. The greatest gift we can give them, is the ability to become responsible adults. This means we must give them enough room to make their own decisions and then live with the consequences of those choices. The more we try to control our teens, the more they will try to assert themselves.

There is simply no way to guarantee that teens will make wise choices. We can only raise the odds that they will make good decisions by providing our thoughts and love, and by helping them see the consequences of heavy mistakes.

Keep communication open— When teens find themselves in difficult situations, they find it helpful to talk to nonjudgmental adults. Being a good listener does not mean you approve of your teen's actions. The more we listen without criticism, the more likely teens are to evaluate their activities.

Limit criticism and restrictions— When we are too critical or restrictive, teens respond with a defensive attitude. They spend more time defending themselves than really thinking about their actions and the possible consequences of those actions. Wise parents are more concerned about their teen's options for handling undesirable activities, than restricting the activities.

Give enforceable rules— Parents are left powerless when they make rules they can't enforce. Enforceable rules deal with issues that directly affect the parents. Grounding is a typical rule many teens refuse to follow.

Let consequences teach—It is tempting to rescue our teens from mistakes. They learn far more valuable lessons by living with the consequences of their actions. A wise parent reacts to their teen's behavior with empathy in place of anger, and allows consequences to do the teaching.

Teens with poor driving records are required to pay for their car insurance. Parents do not allow teens who use drugs or alcohol to drive their cars. Wise parents pay car insurance premiums for those who get good grades, do their chores, and treat their parents with respect.

♥

Let consequences be the "bad guy"
Parents can then be the "good guy"

118

How to Boss Your Kids Around

MANY EXPERTS ARE ENCOURAGING US to replace orders and demands with choices. The odds go up that children will be cooperative, when they feel they have some control over the situation, and this happens when they are offered choices.

Most people have difficulty thinking of choices when their children are giving them trouble. As one mother put it, the only choices she can think of at times like that are, "Hey! Do you want to live or die?"

Needless to say, this is not an effective use of choices. She is in the emotional state at this time, and that is not the best time to try to think of choices.

There are times when we have to give orders or tell children there are no choices. The good news is that we should be able to do this if we are willing to set up a savings account with our children. This is done by giving them choices when everything is going well. Parents who do this effectively are often heard giving choices about things that don't make a lot of difference to them:

- "Do you want to wear red socks, or blue socks?"
- "Do you want to wear your coat, or carry it?"
- "Do you want to eat what is on the table, or wait for the next meal?"
- "Do you want to go to your room with your feet touching the ground, or not touching the ground?"

Then we can make a withdrawal from the savings account when there is a need to give orders.

I met a father who said to me, "Now I understand what my wife has been doing all these years. I always wondered about the routine

she had with the children at bedtime. She may be one of the world's greatest experts on creating a savings account of control. You should hear how she talks with them:"

MOM: "It's time to go to bed. Do you want to go now, or when this TV program is over?"
CHILDREN: "When it's over."
MOM: "Great. You decide. It's your choice."
MOM: "OK, the program is over. Let's go to bed. Do you want a drink of water?"
CHILDREN: "Yeah. We need drinks."
MOM: "Do you want bathroom water, or kitchen water?"
CHILDREN: "Kitchen water!"
MOM: "Good. Do you want it in a cup, or a glass?"
CHILDREN: "A glass."
MOM: "Good decision. Now, do you want a ride down to the bedroom, or do you want to walk on your own?"
CHILDREN: "We want a ride!"
MOM: "Great. Now decide whether you want the light on or off, and whether you want the door shut or open."
CHILDREN: "But we don't want to go to bed!"
This time Mom makes a withdrawal from her savings account.
MOM: "Wait a minute. Didn't you just get to make a whole lot of choices? Don't I get a turn? Well, it's my turn to decide. Thanks for understanding. I'll see you in the morning."

There are times when we must boss our children around. The parents who are able to do this with a minimum of rebellion, are the ones who set the groundwork by having a policy of regularly giving choices when life is going well.

❤

Parents Who Give Choices When Life Is Going Well,
Are Able to Withdraw from Their Savings Account
When There Are No Choices

119

Values: Passing Them on to Our Children

EVERY DAY IT SEEMS THERE'S ANOTHER STORY of the decline in values of our youth in the United States. Drugs are a scourge on the land, available even in remote rural schools. Teenage pregnancy is sky-rocketing. In many schools, teachers are more like police officers than instructors. In our society, proper moral values seem to be taking a pretty good licking.

To parents, this has become a disturbing trend. "I want my children to have responsible moral values," we say. "But how do I teach them those values?"

A great wave of change has swept over our society in the past forty years. The "human rights" revolution has spread, even to our children. Parents cannot make their children think like they do simply by telling them, "You'll do it or else." Demands and threats may yield short-term results, but they don't mold our children's minds. Such tactics don't persuade children that we're right.

Values are passed on to children in two ways: by what children see, and by what they experience in relating to us. When children see us being honest, they learn about honesty. When we talk to our children with love and respect, they learn to talk that way to others.

We can accelerate our modeling of effectiveness by engaging in "eavesdrop value setting." That means that Mom and Dad talk to each other about their values, but within earshot of the children. If we want our children to learn about honesty, for example, we allow them to overhear us reporting on our genuine acts of honesty. "You

know, sweetie," we might say to our spouse. "something interesting happened to me today. At the store I gave the clerk a $5.00 bill for a can of pop and she gave me $14.50 in change. So, I gave her back the ten. I could have said nothing and been $10.00 richer, but I feel so much better being honest—doing what's right."

Children soak up what they hear when we speak to others. It's great when what they soak up is good. Be advised, however, they're sponges for the bad, too.

Our improper words and actions hit them with the same force. If we have nothing but ridicule for our bosses and coworkers, our children learn that ridicule and sarcasm are an acceptable way to talk. If we cheat at board games or when we play sports with our young children, then we shouldn't wring our hands and cry, "Why?" when they get nailed for cheating in school.

The other way we influence our children's values is in the way we treat them. A corollary to the Golden Rule applies here: Children will do to others as their parents do to them. Treating our children with respect teaches them to go and do likewise. Being fair with our children makes them want to be fair to their friends and teachers.

Children have minds of their own. They want to exert their independence and do their own thinking. They shuck off the things that are forced onto them, and embrace the things they want to believe. If we want to pass our values on to them, we must present those values in a way that our children can accept, in our actions and words. A child's values come from what he/she sees and hears—and also overhears. Children don't accept what we try to drive into their heads with lecturing.

Values are passed on by what our children see,
and what they experience in relating to us

Index

Also authored by Jim Fay

Helicopters, Drill Sergeants and Consultants
Toddlers
Trouble-Free Teens
Hormones and Wheels
Love and Logic Solutions
Teaching With Love and Logic

(with Foster W. Cline, M.D.)
Grandparenting With Love and Logic
Parenting With Love and Logic
Parenting Teens With Love and Logic

Order our complete catalog of stress-free
parenting and teaching titles:
1-800-338-4065
or visit us at
www.loveandlogic.com

About the Authors

JIM FAY'S background includes 31 years as a teacher and administrator, 15 years as a professional consultant and public speaker, and many years as a parent of three children.

He serves both nationally and internationally as a consultant to schools, parent organizations, counselors, mental health organizations and the U.S. Military.

Jim is the author of more than 90 articles on parenting and discipline, as well as many audio and video tapes. He has written several books, including *Parenting With Love and Logic* and *Parenting Teens With Love and Logic* (co-authored with Foster W. Cline, M.D.). Both books are recognized by many experts as two of the most practical books ever written on parenting. Jim Fay has also co-authored *Grandparenting With Love and Logic* and *Teaching With Love and Logic*. Jim's delightful sense of humor and his infectious spirit have made him a favorite personality on hundreds of radio and television talk shows.

Jim believes his major accomplishment in life is the development of a unique philosophy (along with Foster W. Cline, M.D.) of practical techniques for enhancing communication between children and adults, known as Love and Logic®. Jim has taken complex problems and broken them down into simple, easy-to-use concepts and techniques which can be understood and used by anyone. Hundreds of thousands of people have expressed how Love and Logic has enhanced their relationshps with their children.

Also authored by Jim Fay

Helicopters, Drill Sergeants and Consultants
Toddlers
Trouble-Free Teens
Hormones and Wheels
Love and Logic Solutions
Teaching With Love and Logic

(with Foster W. Cline, M.D.)

Grandparenting With Love and Logic
Parenting With Love and Logic
Parenting Teens With Love and Logic

Order our complete catalog of stress-free
parenting and teaching titles:
1-800-338-4065
or visit us at
www.loveandlogic.com

ISBN 1-930429-01-0

Library of Congress Card Number: 00-101459

Copyediting: Linda Carlson, Erie, CO
Cover & Book Design: Bob Schram/Bookends, Boulder, CO
Illustration: Joe Howard Studio, Boulder, CO
Project Coordinator: Carol Thomas

Printed in the United States of America

THE
PEARLS
OF
Love and Logic
FOR
PARENTS
AND
TEACHERS

Jim Fay & Foster W. Cline, M.D.

The Love and Logic
PRESS Inc.

www.loveandlogic.com